The End of Overthinking:
Transformative Mindsets to Escape Your Self-Imposed Suffering

By Nick Trenton
www.Nicktrenton.com

Table of Contents

INTRODUCTION — 5

THE WINDOW OF TOLERANCE — 15

COLOR WALKS AND SENSES — 31

SHIFT YOUR LANGUAGE — 41

YOU DON'T NEED TO KNOW EVERYTHING — 57

SHIFT TO PURPOSEFUL MOVEMENT WITH THE DO SOMETHING PRINCIPLE — 69

WONDER INVENTION EXPERIMENTS — 81

DARE METHOD — 93

3-SECOND ANXIETY RELIEF — 107

CHOOSE AGAIN METHOD — 119

BANK OF GOOD THOUGHTS — 127

FOUR-STEP METHOD — 139

THE ANXIETY-CURIOSITY SWITCH — 151

TURN TO PROBLEM-SOLVING 163

ABC COPING SENTENCE 179

GOLDILOCKS PRINCIPLE 187

JOY SPOTTING 199

MANAGE YOUR CORTISOL 211

FEAR-SETTING 225

CONCLUSION 237

Introduction

The overthinker who wants to get better faces some unique challenges:

- Can you think your way out of overthinking?
- Can you force yourself into relaxation?
- Can you fix a broken mind *with* a broken mind?

These questions are certainly a little tongue-in-cheek, but they do reveal something true about how we overcome overthinking: If we hope to be different, we need to try something different.

We need a paradigm shift.

The solution does not lie on the same level as the problem; we need to level up and change how we're thinking about the problem in the first place.

In Jim Rohn's words, **if we want things to change...** ***we*** **have to change.** It's pretty obvious, but also somehow not that simple. We need to have the courage and curiosity to push against what seems automatic, comfortable, or "normal" to us.

Is It Thinking or Overthinking?

The brain is a wonderful thing, and the seat of all of humanity's most impressive feats—communication, creativity, learning, rational problem solving, perception, and understanding, to name a few.

That same organ is also responsible for self-sabotage, delusion, baseless fear, superstition, and lazy habits.

All of these things are "thinking", in their own way.

Let's clarify exactly what we mean by the umbrella term *overthinking*. It covers quite a range of different mental activities, but it's ultimately a question of both the **quality** and the **quantity** of our thoughts.

Here is what overthinking looks and feels like:

- There is a looping, circling, twisting feeling—you keep coming back to the same repetitive thoughts that never seem to go anywhere.
- You feel unable to just *stop*. You can't think of anything else, and you can't not think. The more you try to stop thinking, the more you're thinking about thinking...

- Your thoughts seem to dwell on worst case scenarios, catastrophes, total disasters, and other doom-and-gloom themes.
- You feel mentally exhausted, burned out, and unable to relax.
- You're fixated on risks, threats, fears, failures, and mistakes.
- You delay every decision, overthink it, waffle back and forth indecisively, then choose in panic... and end up regretting everything anyway.
- Your mind keeps replaying situations from the past, or dreaming up situations that may happen in the future.
- You're worried, even (especially?) about those things you can't understand, control, or predict.
- You endlessly rehash old conversations, rehearse future ones, dwell on misfortunes, or fabricate imaginary scenarios that terrify you.
- You get stuck in endless fact-finding, research, and investigation that only leaves you more overwhelmed, confused, and anxious than ever.

How many of these resonate with you?

Overthinkers can feel like their own brains are personal torture devices installed in their heads just to torment them. To make matters worse, plenty of conventional advice centers around things like meditation or challenging your thoughts—which can ultimately make overthinking worse.

The Way Out
Our goal? It's not just to force ourselves to stop overthinking.

Our goal is to *understand* overthinking and rewrite its basic programming from the inside out.

Our goal is not to just eradicate negative thought patterns, but to consciously build new, positive ones. We want to re-learn how to think, feel, and live in ways that are more grounded, balanced, and satisfying.

In this book, we'll be exploring overthinking on several different levels at once:

- Overthinking is a **habit**
    - It's a mental behavior that you've learned; which means you can unlearn it
- Underneath the overthinking habit is an overthinking **mindset**

- - Anxious rumination is not just what you think, it's an attitude
- Underneath the overthinking mindset is a complex set of overthinking **beliefs**
  - These are fundamental views we have towards threat and uncertainty

Your beliefs create your mindset, and your mindset shapes your habits.

The overthinking habit is never superficial. It has deep roots, core beliefs such as:

- "Uncertainty is unacceptable"
- "I am powerless"
- "Anxiety means something is wrong"
- "I am, or should be, in control"
- "I do, or should, know and understand everything"

The guide you're holding in your hands right now is different from other books on the topic because we will be tackling anxiety and overthinking on *all three levels*. We have to handle overthinking at every level, otherwise all of our efforts will amount to little more than temporary symptom relief.

What Causes Overthinking?
A better question might be, *what doesn't?*

Overthinking can be understood as a symptom of a wide range of issues, including:

- Anxiety in general
- Focus and attention issues
- Poor problem-solving skills
- Fear of uncertainty
- Perfectionism
- Panic disorders
- Weak decision-making skills
- Social anxiety
- Low confidence
- Low resilience and poor coping skills
- Trauma and negative life experiences
- Poor physical health

No two people overthink in the same way, or for the same reasons. The overthinking habit can overlap with virtually any mental health disorder, yet is distinct from it.

People may vary in the **target** of their overthinking, for example:

- Health
- Relationships
- Work

- Social life
- Not to mention those big, meaty, existential questions like purpose and meaning

Regardless of the target, the underlying mechanisms are always the same: the **beliefs**, **attitudes,** and **habits** that characterize overthinking.

What This Book Covers
In the chapters that follow, we'll:

- **Explore the HOW and WHY of overthinking,** including:
    - its physiological basis
    - the simple brain switch you can flip to quickly come out of anxiety
    - the fundamental laws of emotional regulation
- **Challenge some misconceptions about stress:**
    - why a little anxiety is actually good for you
    - why approach is better than avoidance
- **Experiment with easy, practical methods** to:
    - regulate our nervous systems and cortisol levels

- consciously shift our perspective
- gently reprogram thought patterns that just aren't working anymore

Though some of these methods and techniques may seem simple at first, their power lies in their *consistent application*. You don't have to fix everything overnight—instead, have faith that easy, modest efforts made every single day are the secret to lasting change.

Overthinking can wreak havoc on your life. It can paralyze you, sap the joy out of your world and twist things so badly you don't know which way is up.

But there's hope: No matter where you are right now, anxiety *does not* have to be a part of your future, and it *does not* have to define you as a person anymore. Overthinking can be overcome, and it doesn't have to be hard work.

Before we dive in, your first task: **Don't overthink your overthinking!**

It's normal.

We all do it now and again.

It won't kill you.

Overthinking is not a sign that you're crazy, that you have a mental illness, that something is wrong in your life, or that you need to embark on a complicated life transformation process before you can feel better again.

In this book, we'll be learning practical ways to dial down anxiety. But the first leap of faith? *Try to feel what it's like to not be anxious about anxiety.*

There's no need to beat yourself up.

You're in the right place.

You're on the right path.

All that's needed now is a little patience, creativity, and self-compassion.

Are you ready?

The Window of Tolerance

"The key to keeping your balance is knowing when you've lost it."

- **Anonymous**

It's 3am. The world outside is dark and still.

But inside your head, everything is moving at 10,000 miles an hour.

You toss and turn, your mind restless, grinding over the same tightening loops again and again until you start wondering if you're genuinely losing it. "Just stop already," you think, but you can't, and then that's another loop, and then you're overthinking the overthinking...

In the morning, you wake up and revisit the Big Scary Thought that kept you up all night. Like a coat on a door that looked like a monster in the dark, this thought suddenly doesn't seem like such a big deal in the light of morning.

The thought is exactly the same, and yet somehow it's not so frightening now as it was last night.

Why?

UCLA clinical professor of psychiatry Daniel J. Siegel has a theory. He talks about The Window of Tolerance, which is essentially a metaphor about nervous system regulation.

- On one side of the window is **hyperarousal**
    - You feel overwhelmed, hypervigilant, wired up, panicky, angry, irritable, confused, and anxious.
    - Your thoughts race and tumble
    - You are out of control
- On the other side of the window is **hypoarousal**
    - You feel shut down, numb, ashamed, flat, defensive, disconnected, depressed, and burned out.
    - Your thoughts are sluggish and foggy
    - You are out of control
- The Goldilocks zone right in the middle is your **window of tolerance**
    - You feel calm, open, curious, grounded, and stable. You're present and emotionally regulated
    - Your thoughts are purposeful, clear, and organized

- You are in control

Hyper- and hypo-arousal are emotional states, but that's not all they are. The thing that is aroused is the nervous system, which means that your entire body is experiencing real, physiological activation.

A cascade of physical reactions is triggered by your autonomic nervous system—increased heart rate, breathing, muscle tension, and blood pressure. In other words, anxiety and overthinking are categorically *not* all in your head. They're all in your body!

Late at night, when your mental and physical resources are depleted, you may slip outside your window of tolerance, so that every minor worry looms over you like the end of the world. In the morning, though, the reset of sleep brings you back to your optimal window, and you can see the problem in proportion again.

The important thing here is not the stimulus, *but our sensitivity to it.*

Overthinking happens when you're in survival mode:

- Hypoaroused - withdrawing and shutting down to protect yourself

- Hyperaroused - anxiously trying to control, fix, or predict things in fight-or-flight mode

If you're inside your window of tolerance, however, your body feels safe enough to process, think through problems, and respond without getting overwhelmed.

Dr. Siegel's theory is useful because it helps us reframe our approach.

Insight 1: You are anxious and overwhelmed not because of the content of your thoughts, but because you're outside your window of tolerance.

Insight 2: Overcoming overthinking is thus about regulating your nervous system, not trying to "think your way out."

When you're in your window of tolerance, you have ready access to your prefrontal cortex, which means you get to use a range of fantastic executive functioning skills:

- Planning
- Analyzing data
- Organizing and prioritizing
- Problem solving
- Decision making and value judgments
- Staying focused

- Managing time
- Setting goals
- Self-discipline
- Resilience
- Communication skills

Life certainly *is* stressful at times, but your brain is a marvelous organ capable of getting you through all sorts of disappointments, challenges, and unexpected turns. That is, if you're in your window of tolerance.

Outside your window, you're no longer thinking, you're surviving. That means you're more inclined to make reckless decisions that backfire, self-sabotage, or get caught in mental ruts that make your life harder, and your relationships more stressful.

Our goals?

- Expand our window of tolerance
- Stay within our window of tolerance as long as possible
- Increase our ability to quickly recover when we *do* slip out of the window

Every one of us has a unique window of tolerance. The parameters may vary depending on our age and stage in life, whether or not we have a trauma history, our personalities, and what's going on for us day to day. It's normal to have to work a little to maintain balance, and it's normal to slip outside of range now and then.

A history of trauma or mental illness can narrow the window, meaning that a trigger that Person A finds manageable may be enough to push Person B into shut-down or anxious rumination. Trauma teaches the body to be over-sensitive to threat. Those of us with trauma backgrounds *can* achieve resiliency and emotional regulation, but we may have to work a little harder at it.

Getting on top of anxiety and overthinking is not a question of cognitive willpower or mental force.

It's not about intellectual understanding.

It's about learning how to give ourselves the support we need for a healthy and well-regulated nervous system.

Thankfully, we have many tools to help widen that window and ensure we're spending as much of our lives inside of it as possible. These tools will come as a surprise to no one:

- Adequate sleep and rest

- Nutritious food
- Exercise and movement
- Meaningful work
- Play, fun, creativity, and enjoyment
- Healthy relationships
- Connection to something greater than ourselves
- Stress management
- Practical environment maintenance—hygiene, life admin, etc.

Our aim is not to *reduce* overthinking and anxiety.

Our aim is to *increase* balance, groundedness, presence, and healthy self-regulation.

IMPORTANT: Being emotionally regulated does *not* mean that we never experience intense emotional arousal. It does not mean we are permanently calm and unflappable. It simply means that we can process our feelings and experiences—whatever they are—healthily and effectively.

Emotional dysregulation often means veering wildly from hyperarousal to hypoarousal. From high-strung to burned out and back again. Frankly, it's hell on the body and mind.

Emotional regulation means finding that smooth, easy path between extremes. You still feel your emotions, but you make fine course corrections and adjustments so that you are never losing control of your awareness or the use of your executive functioning skills.

Sounds nice, but what do you do if you're already emotionally dysregulated?

Step 1: Become aware that you are, in fact, dysregulated.

Step 2: Turn attention away from trying to control the contents of your thoughts and try to find your way back inside the window.

Step 3: Take action accordingly.

Recognizing what is actually happening in your body and your mind is a significant step to taking back control and finding ease and flow again.

Learning how your own window of tolerance works, where its limits are, what pushes you out of it, and what reliably gets you back inside it—these are things anyone can learn with patient practice.

Let's take a look at some practical ways to do just that.

Pay Attention to Your Shifts
Notice your level of regulation all throughout the day—not just when you're feeling overwhelmed.

See if you can catch those early, subtle signs that you are about to drift out of the window.

- **Possible mental signs:** You notice your thoughts become a little obsessive, urgent, tense, impulsive, rigid, or chaotic (hyperarousal), or you notice yourself losing cognitive ability, going blank, or feeling spacey and disconnected (hypoarousal).
- **Possible physical signs:** You notice a sudden tightening of your muscles or breath, an increase in heart rate, sweating, flushing, or shaking (hyperarousal), or you notice a sudden drop in energy, heaviness, slowness, rigidness, and difficulty moving (hypoarousal).
- **Possible behavioral signs**: You notice the urge to do something addictive or impulsive, you experience an emotional outburst/disproportionate reaction (hyperarousal), or you notice a lowered reaction time, autopilot

behavior, and failing to say no (hypoarousal).

Remember that the window is subjective. Everyone's body will send different signs. What's important is that you *identify the shift.* Notice clearly when a change has occurred, even a small one.

For example, you may notice a little flash of irritability, or the sudden impulse to escape or reach for something distracting on your phone. Perhaps you notice yourself sighing and when you tune in to that feeling, you realize you've shifted into a slightly heavier frame of mind.

Identify the Specific Symptoms
Being able to pause and realize, "Wait, something's different," is an excellent first step.

What then?

Try to be precise about what you're feeling, body and mind. Scan yourself emotionally, physically, and mentally. Notice what you're literally *doing*—sometimes our automatic behavior may reveal clues long before our conscious awareness catches up.

The more specific your awareness, the more effective your regulation will be.

Try to identify which side of the window you may be veering towards:

Hyperarousal: shown by an increase in overall energy, movement, heat, and intensity.

Hypoarousal: shown by a decrease in energy and movement. Characterized by blankness, slowness, heaviness, or fogginess.

You might like to keep a journal to record your various mental, emotional, and bodily symptoms as you become aware of them. Record:

- When they happened
- In what context
- How you felt
- Any possible triggers

Over time, you'll uncover certain themes. You'll learn to recognize your own personal tendencies, and the signals that tell you that something is afoot.

Gauge Your Distress Level

One data point to include in your records, if you keep them, is the intensity of the sensation.

When self-awareness is low, we may suffer under quite intense emotional sensations without fully understanding what's going on with us. We may completely miss the warning signs so that it takes a full-blown panic attack for us to consciously register our distress.

By using a ten-point scale, however, we can start to fine-tune our ability to perceive different shades of discomfort, rather than just having two: *OK* and *Problem*. The more sensitively and accurately we can calibrate, the finer the degree of control we have when we self-regulate.

"What is the intensity of this sensation?"

- 1–3: Calm and focused. Comfortably inside the window of tolerance.
- 4–6: Slightly anxious, disconnected, or fatigued. The risk of dysregulation is increased.
- 7–10: Fully reactive, frozen, overwhelmed. Completely outside the window.

It's in that middle 4-6 range, the place where the cart seems to wobble a little on its track, where we need to sit up and pay a little more attention.

Here is where we apply self-regulation tools to get back on track—*before* we head into the 7-10 range.

"What is one small thing I can do right now to reset?"

If you catch minor wobbles while they're still minor, then you don't have to do as much work to bring yourself back into balance.

- Take a break
- Go for a walk
- Have a sip of water
- Do a quick breathing exercise
- Grab a snack
- Check in with a friend
- Do some stretches

A good rule of thumb is to take action that counters your current energy state. If you're feeling hypoaroused and at risk of shutting down, for instance, then you might go for a brisk walk outside in the fresh air to get your blood pumping and your muscles moving.

On the other hand, if you're feeling hyperaroused, take some slow, deep breaths, close your eyes, and focus on a mantra or simple mental image to slow your thoughts.

Identify What Triggered the Shift
Once you've identified a shift, gauged it, and taken gentle counteraction, then you're in the position to ask,

"What just happened?"

Once you're feeling calm and in the window again, it's a good idea to look back and identify what set you off in the first place.

Don't be too quick to assume what the trigger was; it's not always what you think. For example, you may have suddenly snapped at a loved one, and realized you were slightly hyperaroused. But why?

It's not because they were being especially annoying. Rather, after a little investigation, you may realize that you were feeling annoyed several minutes *before* the outburst, because of something completely unrelated.

Trying to pinpoint real triggers takes time, honesty, and self-compassion.

If you can run through each of these steps every time you begin to shift out of your window of tolerance, you'll teach yourself to notice early warning signs of stress, intervene sooner, and as a result, stay within your window more of the time. You'll be less reactive, less prone to rumination, and less likely to wear yourself out with overthinking and anxiety.

Color Walks and Senses

"When there are thoughts, it is distraction. When there are no thoughts, it is meditation."

- **Ramana Maharshi**

When you were little, did your parents ever encourage you to play a game of "I spy" while on long car trips?

There was a reason: They wanted to distract you so that you wouldn't be fighting with your siblings or asking, "Are we there yet?" hundreds of times.

Where your attention goes, the rest of you follows; so, if your attention is happily engaged with *external* stimuli, then that means it's not hyper-focused on some *internal* worry (like... are we there yet?).

"Color walks" work on the same principle: **strategic and playful distraction.**

Once overthinking is underway, it becomes a little like a perpetual motion machine. It can feel impossible to stop... so don't stop. Just redirect.

Put your attention elsewhere.

No force is needed for this—in fact, you can completely come away from an obsessive worry with just a little playful, curious attention directed somewhere else.

Be like your own parent and give your stressed-out mind a little job to do.

The game goes like this: Pick a color, then head out on a walk and see how many things you can spot that are that color. Easy.

The color walk's beauty lies in its simplicity:

- It's fun but not madly overstimulating.
- It gently shifts your focused awareness in an open-ended way, which means you come out of flight-or-flight mode and into hopeful exploration mode.
- Finally, it's logically impossible to be engrossed in *two* fully absorbing tasks at the same time, so switching attention completely knocks the steam out of any rumination loops you may be stuck in.

Without you even realizing it, a color walk can bring you into a state of mindfulness where you are anchored in your senses (in the here and now) rather than in the endless maze of your own thoughts.

You can always change the rules of the game as you go along.

Maybe you want to *count* the number of items you spot.

Maybe you want to stick strictly to the exact hue you've chosen, or maybe you're just looking for anything in any shade of blue.

Maybe you ask a friend to join.

You can make the walk as long as you like, and you can opt for a city stroll or a nature walk in the park or woods.

It's up to you. Outdoor walks already come with a host of health benefits that are hard to overstate:

- "Walking decreases the risk or severity of various health outcomes such as cardiovascular and cerebrovascular diseases, type 2 diabetes mellitus, cognitive impairment and dementia, while also improving mental well-being, sleep, and longevity" (Ungvari, et. al., 2023).
- Walking (like any physical activity) improves blood pressure, lipid and

cholesterol levels, body composition, mental health, osteoporosis, aerobic power, and orthopedic problems (Davidson & Grant, 1993).
- Walking improves mood and may relieve symptoms of depression (Robertson et al., 2012, Biddle et. al., 2015).
- Walking may have far-reaching benefits for creativity, personal reflection, and social wellbeing (Solnit, 2001).
- Walking may also help with anxiety, since it "might help us feel better because we are in control of doing something good for ourselves or we can see progress in our abilities or simply distract us from things that are causing us stress or anxiety" (Biddle, Mutrie & Gorely, 2015).

The trouble is, going on a long walk in beautiful nature won't help you much if you spend every minute of it ruminating anxiously. If you are beating yourself up with negative self-talk, stewing over past events, or dreading future ones, you may be *physically* walking, but you're not present enough to derive any *psychological* benefits from the activity.

Adding the color game to your walks will help you **stay grounded and present** in what you're doing. By consciously redirecting your awareness, you activate your parasympathetic nervous system—that is, "rest and digest" mode—and bring more balance and flow.

Be present.

Slow down.

Notice your surroundings—in detail.

Adopt the fun and anticipation of an "Easter egg hunt" mentality—what surprises lay in wait for you? Where could they be?!

Color walks are a wonderful and highly effective alternative for those who find formal meditation hard going. When you are hyperaroused and already caught in an overthinking spiral, sitting down to meditate can be counterproductive, paradoxically dialing up cognitive noise.

Overthinkers often sit down to meditate, notice their thought traffic, then try to forcefully stop or control it, launching themselves into spirals of shame, annoyance... and more anxiety.

But you don't have to do this.

Just *redirect* the thought processes by giving your brain an easy sensory task.

We've all been told that distraction is bad, but remember that not all distractions are created equal.

Notice if you do have the urge to reach for a distraction, such as:

- Scrolling aimlessly on your phone
- Shopping or browsing online
- Gaming
- Binge eating

These things may bring temporary relief for an over-busy brain, but they're not healthy or sustainable in the long run. Instead, be kind to the impulse when you notice it arise—see it as a sign that your brain needs a break from itself—and redirect to a gentler, healthier distraction, like a color walk.

Engage All Your Senses While Moving

What if you live in a really gray urban environment?

What if you're limited in how much walking you can do?

That's no problem. You can still use the principle of strategic distraction.

For example, engage your other senses:

- **Hearing** – Count how many distinct sounds you hear when on your walk, or even when sitting at a window or a back garden. Listen to the volume of sounds, and try to rank the loudest to the quietest. What's the *tiniest* sound you can hear?
- **Touch** – cancan you spot any notable textures (of course you don't have to literally touch things)? How many smooth, rough, furry, metallic things you can find? Can you feel the breeze on your skin? What's the consistency of the ground beneath you? Does it change?
- **Smell** – Notice what you can smell. Really tune in—do you notice how even the air in your nostrils has a very faint scent?
- **Sight** – If colors aren't your thing, notice variations that exist between how an object appears in shade versus sunlight. Notice the shapes of different objects, look for different fonts on storefront signs, spot flower or tree species, notice dogs and other animals, or see how many manhole covers you can find along the road.

- **Taste** – This one may be a little trickier, but consider a forest walk where you scout out the foliage and decide whether you could potentially eat this or that, and what it might taste like if you did. (Obligatory warning: Don't literally go tasting things you find in the forest!)

You get the idea.

In reality, it doesn't matter which of your senses you engage, or what precise task you absorb yourself in. What matters is that you're *not* being absorbed by what's whirling around in your own mind.

Use Creative Variations When Needed

Making up variations of the color walk idea is a game in itself.

Why not try a different variation every time you step out for a stroll?

Even the most seemingly barren environment may yield a sense of fun and discovery with the right prompt. Keep your games fairly simple, and make sure you're staying firmly *outside* your head, not inviting yourself further in.

The groundedness of this exercise comes from engaging with your environment, so try to avoid the temptation to disappear into your own thoughts.

- **Try an alphabet walk**. This is where you find objects that begin with each letter of the alphabet, in order.
- **Find a tactile anchor.** Pick up a stone, pebble, leaf, or pinecone and let your fingers explore it as you walk. Feel every nook and cranny, note its texture, weight, and heat.
- **Try people watching.** See if you can spot five people with red hair, a woman with a boy and a girl child, or a man with a blue shirt and a dog, for example.

Before you head out on your walk, pause to do a quick body scan and check in with your emotions.

What are you feeling?

What is the intensity of those feelings?

Can you identify the main characteristics of your thought process?

When you come back from your sensory walk, check in with yourself again, and compare.

Do you feel calmer or more grounded?

Shift Your Language

"The magic of each day lives in the unknown. It's waking up as one person, and accepting that when night falls, we may be someone else entirely. So, when you ask what my story is, forgive me—I'm not quite sure yet."

- J. Raymond

Overthinking can be difficult to let go of because it *feels* like it's an important and necessary thing to do.

Essentially, **overthinking is a problem trying to disguise itself as a solution.**

Overthinking may feel like a legitimate path to a solution, but it isn't. Instead, it's your brain anxiously elaborating on its own attempts to control the uncontrollable, predict the unpredictable, or change the unchangeable.

Let's say you're worried about a presentation you're about to give. You know the material, you're prepared, and you've given dozens of similar presentations in the past.

But your brain tosses out that tired old chestnut that begins: "What if...?"

What if you run out of time?

What if there's a person in the audience who asks a question you can't answer?

What if you suddenly panic and faint right in the middle of your speech, in front of everyone?

What if...?

What if...?

What if...?

You try to stop your anxious train of thought, but you can't. Why? Because your brain has tricked you into thinking that the endless scenarios it's spinning are in some way helpful. There might be a threat, and your brain is going to uncover it for you and keep you safe. Isn't that a good thing?

After all, what if you relax now but regret it later?

What if everything you're worrying about happening really *does* happen...?

What if...

There it is again. Those two little words that can completely destroy your peace of mind.

Think about these two little words for a moment. *What if.* They do not point to a genuine question. Rather, these two words invite you to open up the door for an infinite number of awful possibilities to rush in.

There is no real way to *answer* such a non-question, is there?

Entertaining a scary possibility doesn't help you clarify the likeliness of it happening. It doesn't help you prepare for it. It doesn't help you manage it when/if it arrives.

All these two words do is trigger a little bubble of irresolvable anxiety. That's all.

Well, that's not all, actually. Every "what if" question tends to push you to ask three more.

This is the kind of question that encourages you to think passively, to focus on threat, to go into reactive panic mode, and to forget your own agency and responsibility in any given scenario.

A slight shift in language changes everything:

Say "We'll see," instead.

- You pivot out of apathy and fear and into acceptance.
- You stop. You come to the present. You rest.
- You calm your nervous system. There's nothing you need to figure out, nothing to uncover or resolve, no menacing possibilities lurking somewhere for you to uncover.
- You move from what might happen to what *is* happening, right now—and what you might do next.

What if has no natural termination point. It has no guardrails built in.

We'll see is small, manageable, and final.

What if says you're never really finished worrying.

We'll see says we've done what we can, now we can rest. The outcome will be what it will be.

Here's how a gentle shift in language can help shift your mindset, and help you get unstuck:

Replace "What if?" with "We'll see."
Hypotheticals are useless.

Truly, they serve precisely zero function in your life.

A hypothetical is a house of cards built on a cloud. It's even less than that.

- *What if they laugh at me?*
    - They might. They might not. You won't know until it happens. So why not wait and see?
- *What if I offended her yesterday?*
    - Maybe you did. Maybe you didn't. You won't know until you know. So why not wait and see?
- What if my date tomorrow flops and I never get another one and I'm doomed to spend the rest of my life alone with nobody but Mittens and Mr. Meatball for company?
    - Hey, that really might happen. But be fair—can you really make definitive conclusions about your *entire life* when you haven't actually lived it yet? So why not wait and see?

The anxious mind will try to convince you that there's something you can do right now to prevent the bad thing happening... but is that true? It might try to tell you that your rumination right now can somehow help you travel back into the past and change things... but can you?

When you say, "We'll see," you collapse the infinite universe of awful possibilities down to what is actually in your control. Instead of getting caught in a panic spiral that you sent a poorly written email, you can just say to yourself, "I communicated my message as clearly as I knew how. We'll see how it lands."

Let's look at some more examples:

- "I studied and I did my best on the exam. We'll see what grade I get."
- "I submitted my application. It's too late to change it now. We'll see if I get in."
- "I've been honest about my feelings, and that's all I can do. We'll see how he responds."

See how different that feels?

Reset, ground in the present, and remind yourself that the future is, after all, entirely out of your control.

Stop Replaying the Past Unless It's Changed

Maybe your "What if" demon doesn't use future hypotheticals as his preferred torture device, but instead subjects you to questions about the past.

- You made a decision yesterday—but what if you've made a massive mistake?
- That party yesterday was awkward as hell—what if they were all talking about you?
- Your childhood memories are kind of fuzzy—what if this is actually a really serious case of traumatic amnesia and your entire family is hiding the truth from you?!

The anxious mind can project an unlimited variety of imaginary monsters into the future, and it can do the same trick with the past.

But why does it do this?

It's simple: **Uncertainty is uncomfortable.**

An issue may be completely resolved, dead and buried in the past, but if we are *psychologically* unable to let it go, it hangs around and haunts us.

Importantly, this feeling of psychological closure is not about the situation at hand. *It's about us.*

Earlier, we spoke about the window of tolerance, but we didn't cover what exactly we are meant to be tolerating when in this window.

A big part of distress tolerance is uncertainty tolerance.

- The brain craves certainty, predictability, control, and ease.
- Real life gives it uncertainty, unpredictability, vulnerability, and struggle.

How do we resolve the discrepancy?

The anxious mind tells us: "Find more information! Go and rehash the past over and over until it makes sense! Try to force a conclusion. If we worry enough, we'll figure this out, I'm sure of it."

A calm, rational mind says something different: "What's done is done. I don't have perfect knowledge, and I never will. I can accept that. I've done what I can, and I'm OK with a bit of ambiguity."

Reviewing mistakes is what allows us to learn and grow. Observe outcomes, adjust, try again, and keep going.

But *rumination*? That's just spinning your wheels.

Try to observe a new rule with yourself: **"I will not revisit an event from the past unless some new information in the present demands it."**

Your brain will want to return to a prior decision or a past event simply because it's uncomfortable with uncertainty and wants to find a way to resolve that uncertainty. Spoiler alert: Revisiting the past does not reduce uncertainty. Ruminating over the past will leave you in precisely the same position as you are now, only more anxious.

Analysis of the past only makes sense if more data comes your way. If not, that means you're no longer analyzing—you're ruminating.

- Breathe
- Notice that you're ruminating
- Draw a mental line under the past, and your ruminating
- Say, "That's done," and believe yourself

- File the past away. Even if it's incomplete, or a little messy, or contains a few uncomfortable holes that you wish you could fill in. Just file it away as it is. Yes, it's not perfectly resolved. File it away anyway, in that uncertainty.
- Redirect your focus to the present and all the things you actually can influence

Example: Your date ghosted you. You don't know why, and maybe you never will. That's OK. Hold that uncertainty. You don't need to figure anything out, or make sense of it, or explain it.

You don't need to make up a big story about it and tell yourself that story on an endless loop.

Just file it in the "It's done" cabinet and move on.

Of course, if six months later your missing date re-appears with something they want to tell you, that's a different story! That's new information that gives you a reason to look back into the past if you choose to.

Ask: "Am I Solving, or Just Circling?"

I'm going to say something that may sound a little harsh: Sometimes, we are reluctant to give up an overthinking habit because deep down we hold the unconscious belief that overthinking is kind of… smart.

Let me put it another way. We picture a happy-go-lucky, relaxed personality and agree that it must be nice to live like that. And yet…

- We hear "accepting" and interpret it to mean "resigned."
- We hear "relaxed" and think "lazy."
- We hear "contentment" and assume it means "low standards."

Basically, many of us hold onto the overthinking habit because we sincerely find it useful. We believe, on a very deep level, that it's not only a handy tool, but an *essential* tool—that we simply could not navigate life without it.

We may have convinced ourselves that smart, responsible, and put-together people are necessarily strung out.

We believe that overthinking = thinking.

We may lie to ourselves:

"Oh, I'm not overthinking, I'm just...

- "Preparing"
- "Researching"
- "Planning"
- "Processing"
- "Problem solving."

But are you? Are you really?

Real talk: You cannot fully drop the overthinking habit unless you can see it for what it really is.

Not everything that you do with your brain is useful.

Not all thinking is helpful.

Just because you're in your head doesn't mean you're doing something smart, productive, or healthy.

How can we tell the difference?

Healthy, productive thoughts:

- Are linear—they go somewhere
- Instigate healthy, concrete action
- Stop when the job is done

Unhealthy, unproductive thoughts:

- Are loopy, repetitive, disorganized—they spiral and go nowhere

- Prevent healthy, concrete action
- Never stop

Healthy, productive thought is like the motion of a finely engineered car. It's powerful but controlled. The engine starts when you turn the ignition key and stops when you turn it off. In between, you steer the car along your route in a neat, defined line until you reach your destination. The car then sits and waits quietly until you need it again.

Unhealthy, unproductive thought is like the motion of a car stuck in the mud. There's power and noise and plenty of force, but *you're not moving*. You're using up gas, you're burning out your tires, and mud's flying everywhere. The tires are spinning and you're certainly clocking miles... but you're not exactly driving, are you?

Get into the habit of asking yourself whether you're *thinking* or *overthinking*.

- If you're worried about an upcoming meeting, ask yourself: "Am I actually *preparing* for this, or am I just imagining all the ways it could go wrong?"

- If you're stewing over a mistake you made, ask yourself, "Am I really *learning* from this, or am I just beating myself up?"
- If you're trying to navigate a complicated challenge, ask yourself, "Am I really *researching* and *problem-solving*, or am I just catastrophizing?"

There are two main ways to respond to any dilemma life can throw your way.

Yes, really. Just two:

- Change things
- Accept things

"Can I change anything here?"

You may be able to influence things 100%, only somewhat, or not at all. Decide what small, concrete step you *can* take right now (and don't get distracted by the fact that this number may not be as high as you'd like).

- Tighten up your presentation notes if you know they could objectively use some work.
- Journal the insights you've gained from the mistake, then take action right now to be better.

- Book the earliest doctor's appointment you can, then stop googling your symptoms.

"If I *can't* change anything here, what can I do to accept it?"

Accepting something doesn't mean you agree with it, like it, or want it to continue. It just means you acknowledge that it's not currently in your control. It's an agreement with yourself that you will not argue with reality.

- Distract yourself
- Redirect your attention to something that's going well
- Engage in a little self-care

The more often you replace speculation and useless mental angst with acceptance, the more energy you free up for what actually matters.

"We'll see." is a way to reclaim your energy.

"It's done." is a boundary you set with yourself.

"I've done what I can; I accept the rest." is a motto for freedom and relief.

You Don't Need to Know Everything

"You don't have to figure everything out today. You don't have to solve your whole life overnight. And you don't have to tackle everything at once. You just have to show up and try. You just have to focus on the most immediate thing in front of you. And you just have to trust that you'll figure out the rest along the way."

- Danielle Koepke

Let's return to the concept of uncertainty tolerance and dig a little deeper.

What are we really saying, when we say that we cannot tolerate uncertainty?

To paraphrase a little, it means we don't know, yet **we believe we should know.**

- We don't know the answer
- We don't understand
- We don't know the outcome
- We don't know what to do
- *And we don't like it*

Let's pause and get a little philosophical about this.

The above attitude is a kind of mental orientation to reality that is *bound to* create anxiety. Literally, that is its most predictable byproduct.

We don't know, but believe we should; therefore, we feel distressed. Where does the distress come from in this equation?

The not knowing?

Or the belief that we *should*?

An alternative: Socratic ignorance

For the sake of argument, let's invert the above attitude:

- We don't know the answer
- We don't understand
- We don't know the outcome
- We don't know what to do
- *And we are 100% OK with that*

Our level of ignorance stays the same, we just change the way we think about that ignorance.

Socrates famously said, "I know only one thing: that I know nothing."

This is a philosophical proposition, but it's also an expression of a particular mindset and way of being.

Socrates was considered wise, but the foundation of this wisdom was humility, and the honest acknowledgment of how little he knew about the deeper truths of reality. In Socrates' dialogues, rigorous questioning always reveals that people know less than they think they do.

This is an important point. Not only is our baseline state generally one of ignorance, but even when we feel that we do know something... we're often deluding ourselves.

Thus Socrates often questioned people on the basics of their understanding, only to reveal that the basis of their certainty and understanding was actually an illusion.

There are two paradoxical ideas here:

- Faulty or untested beliefs can supply the *illusion* of knowledge
- On the other hand, our most secure and truthful position may be one of total confession: *"Maybe I know nothing after all."*

You don't have to get embroiled in philosophical thought to understand how the quest for certain knowledge can be a trap. Trying to predict, control, and understand everything can ironically make us more ignorant and inaccurate than ever.

Socrates said: **"Awareness of ignorance is the beginning of wisdom."**

Let's adjust this for our own purposes: **Acceptance of ignorance is the beginning of serenity.**

Socrates used epistemic doubt to shape his search for true wisdom and knowledge.

This was his philosophical position.

We can apply a little of this sentiment in our own lives.

- Anxiety says: I need to know. I have to know.
- Serenity says: I don't know. It's OK that I don't know.

This can be our psychological position.

Instead of fearing uncertainty, we can embrace it with humility and curiosity.

Why not stop pretending that we have the answers?

Why not let go of the pressure to have everything all figured out?

Why not stop punishing ourselves for not knowing?

It's not about being passive, but shifting out of a controlling, obsessive, and perfectionist frame of mind. We don't have to be in control, and we don't have to understand everything perfectly all at once.

The irony is that when we relax and give ourselves permission to not know… we truly open up to learning. That means that giving ourselves permission to not know is the only process that reliably helps us to know more!

Ask Yourself: "What Don't I Know Yet?"
It's not a bad thing to reflect.

However, *anxious* reflection—overthinking—stems from the belief that we should already know. As a result, this kind of thinking is actually focused on the shame, discomfort, and awkwardness of not knowing, and the desire to escape that uncomfortable feeling as quickly as possible.

We are no longer driven by curiosity or a sincere desire to improve, discover, or learn. We just feel that our current lack of understanding is unpleasant, and we want it to stop. Big difference!

It's OK to be in process.

It's OK for things to take time.

It's OK to know some things, but to not know others (yet... or ever).

To encourage productive reflection, try journaling according to the following prompts:

- What assumptions have I made today?
- What didn't go as I expected it to?
- What questions do I still have?

This turns reflection into a tool for insight, not shame.

Challenge Your Thoughts Like Socrates Would

Is your mind spiraling?

Apply the Socratic method on yourself. Start up a dialogue with your own thought processes and question everything.

Here are some questions that will steer you away from uncertainty-phobia and towards serenity, acceptance, and productive thinking:

- Is this absolutely true?
- What evidence do I actually have for thinking this?

- What am I afraid is going to happen, anyway?
- What would I tell a friend who thought this?
- Is there another way to think about this?
- What assumptions am I making?

For example, let's say you're facing a possible new house purchase. It's a big decision, and there's a lot of money on the line. Your anxious brain might keep pushing you to focus on all the terrifying unknowns.

You don't really know what it will be like to live in this house. You don't know about all the potential problems not disclosed by the sellers. You don't know if the price is too high or if it will get higher in the future. You don't know much about your neighbors, or what will be built across the road in ten years' time. You don't know if you'll regret buying this house, or if you'll regret *not* buying it…

Your anxious brain's solution? Go into a panic and try to find all this out.

That means staying up all night anxiously "researching." Far beyond the point of due diligence, you stew over questions you cannot possibly answer.

Your brain's proposed solution seems like a good idea, but it isn't. Instead, try Socratic dialogue:

Anxious brain: "This is life or death. I can't mess this decision up."

Calm brain: "Hang on. Is that really true? Like, 100% true?"

AB: "Well, I don't *want to* mess it up."

CB: "OK. But what do you mean, mess it up? What are you really afraid of?"

AB: "Well, maybe there's black mold in the living room and they're lying about it."

CB: "Do you have any evidence to think that?"

AB: "Well, no. But still, if it turns out buying this house is a big, fat, mistake, then…"

CB: "Then what?"

AB: "Then… it'll be awful. I'll hate that."

CB: "And then what?"

AB: "Then what? Well, I don't know. It'll be a disaster. I'll have to sell it again I guess."

CB: "Is that really so bad?"

AB: "…"

1. This kind of inner dialogue is not about inviting further overthinking. It's about shifting out of repetitive loops and getting real with yourself about What you actually know
2. What you need to know

Sit with the Question and Don't Rush the Answer

Overthinking is sometimes just a symptom of impatience.

It's normal to ask questions or to seek understanding.

But that doesn't mean that the answers have to be instant, nor does it mean they have to come to us exactly on our terms.

We need to learn to increase our tolerance for that passage of time between question and answer. Clarity and understanding might be instantaneous, but it's far more likely that it will take a few minutes, days, weeks, or even longer..

Have the discipline to hold an unanswered question without rushing to force a premature resolution.

Observe your thoughts without demanding closure.

Remind yourself that not all problems need immediate solutions, and that you only stress yourself out by expecting them.

What does "sitting with" uncertainty really look like, in the real world? Let's imagine that you've raised a question about mold in the new house, and investigations are underway. You've done all you can, but now you have to wait for the outcome.

You're still worried though.

1. Notice the anxious thought as it pops up ("What if there's mold in the house?")
2. Label it, without shame or blame ("Ah, here's that doubt and fear again.")
3. Now, don't do anything. There's no need to fix it, and there's also no need to forcefully try to accept it. Just be still, present *with* the doubt and fear.
4. If you notice an impulse to escape ("Let me just look up some stats about mold online...") gently stop yourself and redirect.
5. Tell yourself: **"I don't need to resolve uncertainty to be safe."** Try to find that feeling of safety *alongside* the fear and doubt.

With repeated practice, this process will build your uncertainty tolerance.

You will teach your mind that there really is nothing to worry about. That you can comfortably live a rich and fulfilling life that's full of unknowns.

Do what you can to find answers, then relax in the rest. Your goal is not to attain some state of perfect knowing, it's to skillfully navigate the path you need to walk to get to that knowing.

Shift to Purposeful Movement with the Do Something Principle

"Nothing diminishes anxiety faster than action."

- **Walter Anderson**

Overthinking is often just ordinary decision-making caught in a loop.

Here's what ordinary decision making might look like:

1. You plan, research, and ask questions.
2. You come to a decision.
3. You take action.
4. The end.

And here's what overthinking might look like:

1. You plan, research, and ask questions.
2. Repeat step 1.
3. You come to a decision.
4. You take action.
5. The end.

It's the same basic process… but overthinking has created a perpetual loop right at step 1.

Action is the secret ingredient that gets things moving, but if you loop and loop before you get to that step, then you never reach the point where you can say "I'm done here." and move on.

Author of *Do It Tomorrow and Other Secrets of Time Management* Mark Forster explains that there are two modes:

1. Thought → Decision → Action (chilled out, productive)
2. Stimulus → Reaction (anxious)

Let's imagine that a big speeding fine has suddenly appeared in the mail. Let's imagine you're in the chilled out, productive mode. How do you respond?

Answer: You quickly read the document, figure out how much you have to pay, and maybe go online to quickly resolve the payment and get that monkey off your back. If you are on a tight schedule and don't have the time, you immediately make a note on your phone to settle the fine when you get home later that day.

You thought about it, you made a decision, you took action. You got on with your day.

Done. The end.

What does it look like in the other, anxious mode?

Answer: You immediately read the document and freak out. Instantly you're stewing over the unfairness of the fine, you're complaining loudly to people around you, you're worrying about how you're going to afford it, you're scheming clever ways to get out of it, you're worrying about how much jail time there might be for people who dodge speeding fines…

Because you're bumbling with this, you're late out the door to your next commitment. This only results in more stress. You get home later and remember the fine, but you can't remember where you put it. You do another task—poorly, because you're still ruminating over the fine. Stress continues to ramp up. The next day you forget all about the fine (a new crisis has taken your attention) until the end of the month when you get a follow-up letter that includes the same fine and a hefty late fee on top of it.

There's a lot of activity here, but no conscious action. You just reacted. There was a stimulus, you reacted, there was another one, you reacted to that, and so on and so on. You're stuck at step 1, eternally reacting and never giving yourself the chance to decide, and take action.

Overthinking sometimes means underdoing.

You're caught in a reactive stress loop that actually gets you nowhere. This explains why there's often a link between:

- Poor time management
- Anxiety and overthinking
- Procrastination and avoidance

Productivity guru Mark Manson has a slightly different take, which he calls the "Do Something" principle.

It's about disrupting the cycle and **shifting from perfect decisions to immediate actions.**

With overthinking, we dawdle and linger in uncertainty and fear. We get stuck in information-gathering loops and endless conjecture and guesswork. But Manson asks us to imagine things the other way around: Don't wait for clarity, create it.

How? By taking action.

When you act and do something—anything—you break out of your overthinking inertia and give yourself some fresh data to work with. You get moving again.

While Forster's model is:

>Thought → Decision → Action

Manson's model cuts to the chase even quicker:

>**Action** → Thought → Decision → Action

When you take action first, you simply don't allow yourself to fall into rumination loops or endless introspection.

Dean Bokhari puts it this way: "It's easier to act yourself into a better way of feeling than it is to feel yourself into a better way of acting."

By starting with action, you terminate anxious overthinking loops before they've even begun, and set up healthier, more productive loops instead:

>Action → Motivation → More action → More motivation...

Whichever model makes sense to you, one thing is clear: Action dispels the inertia of overthinking.

Remember: Action over thinking, not overthinking action.

Make the Decision Once—So You Don't Re-Decide Daily

One way to break the stagnation of overthinking is to improve your ability to make decisions by making them promptly.

Another way is to take the decision off your plate entirely and relegate it to the category of "rule" or "habit." If something is a rule or a habit, you don't have to repeatedly decide to do it. It just gets done.

For example, you may find that keeping on top of emails and messages is stressful and overwhelming, and a major source of overthinking for you. Instead of having to decide day after day to tackle your inbox, just make a rule: "I respond to emails every day at 4pm."

This is a pre-decision that lowers the amount of energy needed to just take action. There's nothing to overthink—you don't need to revisit anything, plan anything, convince yourself of anything, or get caught up in endless self-negotiations.

You respond to emails at 4pm, and that's that.

Is it 4pm? Then you respond to emails.

- The thinking has already been done
- The decision has already been made
- All that's left for you is to take **action**

Pre-decisions of this kind put useful behaviors on autopilot, removing the friction that overthinking thrives on.

Shrink the Task Until It Feels Too Small to Overthink

Overthinking feeds on complexity.

If you make things ultra-simple, however, there's nothing to overthink.

For example, you may need to file your taxes. You've been putting it off because your overthinking mind has latched onto the many separate steps involved... plus added a few more steps that aren't.

If you shrink the task down and just focus on the first or simplest step, that sense of complexity disappears. Tell yourself that your task is simply that first teeny, tiny step. And I really do mean tiny:

- Clarifying the deadline
- Gathering your bank statements, even if it's just one

- Filling your name and address on the first page

Just pick one tiny thing. *That's all.* That's the whole task.

If you find your mind trying to chip in with objections and second-guesses, remind it:

"My goal is not to do the whole thing. My goal is just to get started."

Then just focus on that next step. Not much to do. Not much to think about.

But once you take action, then you're moving. Suddenly, the pressure is off. You don't have to experience the anxiety of procrastination because—ta da! —you are already doing the task.

The smaller the action, the easier it is to get unstuck and moving again.

And the sooner you can start moving, the sooner you can stop ruminating.

Lower the Bar and Take Imperfect Action Anyway

Do you remember when you were a kid, and you were teetering on the edge of a pool, trying to coax yourself to just jump already? Or maybe you were trying to gather the courage to go down a scary-looking waterslide, or leap out of a tree.

Whatever it was for you, I'm positive you know the feeling I'm talking about: hesitant, doubtful, and *madly anxious*. It's like there's a wall in front of you.

Once you jump, though, everything changes. And it changes quickly!

Yes, hitting that ice-cold water or whizzing down the water slide may be a sudden and thrilling rush, but the *anxiety* is gone—you have taken action, and you are swiftly being carried along by the momentum of that action.

We face similar moments like this all throughout life.

- We write and rewrite the same email ten times, unable to just send it already.
- We spend countless mental hours rehearsing a little speech we want to say to someone, unable to just rip the band aid off and say what we need to.
- We procrastinate taking an important step because we don't feel "ready" yet, but the more we wait, the less ready we feel.

There's that wall again.

Overthinking is hesitation. And what are we waiting for, exactly?

We're holding back, doubting, delaying, all because we think we cannot act until there's some guarantee of perfection, of total knowledge, or of complete clarity and understanding. We tell ourselves we can't act until we feel safe, fully in control, and in complete possession of every last fact and detail.

So we stand there on the precipice, dithering.

The solution is not to say, "yes, yes, I'm terrified now, but in just a minute I'll feel differently, and I'll jump in then."

The solution is to **take action now, even if that action is imperfect.**

Uncertainty isn't dangerous, it's part of the process.

The irony is that once you take that leap, everything changes anyway. The clarity you were wanting suddenly catches up with you.

You're completely submerged in the pool.

You're whizzing down the slide.

You've landed beneath the tree.

You're on the other side of the wall.

Taking action works precisely because it short circuits all the core beliefs underpinning the overthinking habit.

- You don't need to be motivated
- You don't need to be fearless
- You don't need to have it all figured out
- You don't need massive insight or a big breakthrough
- You don't need to find it easy
- You don't need to be ready
- You don't need to be perfect

You just need to take action, and get yourself on the path. You'll figure things out on the way, in due course.

Action halts rumination cycles because it's not motivational or psychological—it's mechanical. Just *move*.

Progress over paralysis.

Remember: Mind follows motion.

Wonder Invention Experiments

"Wonder is seeing things the way you saw them before they became ordinary."

- **Nate Staniforth**

Overthinking is about the illusion of control.

It's a fear-based reaction to uncertainty and the vulnerability of being in process.

When you're overthinking, all you want is clarity, resolution, and *control*. At the root of all anxiety is the desire to be in charge, to predict, and to manage the chaos and unpredictability of life...

But did you know that **overthinking stifles creativity?** Innovation, play, novelty, and out-of-the-box thinking come from chaos and unpredictability!

The desire to control shrinks our world. It's like walking through a vast and wondrous forest, but stressing about staying exactly on the footpath, closely following the map you have in your head, and never lifting your gaze long enough to ask, "Hey, what's down *that* path?"

If we want to be in complete control and have full knowledge, then we shut out the possibility of being surprised by something we don't yet know.

If you gaze out at this forest and can't help but overthink every single possible path ahead of you, you may experience overwhelming analysis paralysis, and never take that first step.

In both instances, we are caught in a kind of **rigidity**. Stuck in analyzing, predicting, and mentally spiraling so that every tiny choice feels like a big deal.

In fact, there's now evidence that this is not just a psychological phenomenon, but a neurological one: When the right frontal pole of the brain is overstimulated, creative expression is dampened and perfectionism and tunnel vision increase (Kutsche et. al., 2025).

Your right frontal pole is responsible for:
- Controlled decision making
- Self-reflection
- High level executive functioning

Stimulation in this area is good… but too much can lead to overthinking and overwhelm. The result is the self-censorship of new and unconventional ideas. In other words, when we're overwhelmed and processing too much, our brain actually steps in and clamps down on our creativity.

To cut a long story short, **if you're in overthinking mode, you're making it harder for yourself to be in creative mode.**

The overthinking habit and the attitude of rigid control are two sides of the same coin. We may flip between both; one moment entertaining a thousand amazing new ideas all at once, the next feeling burned out and frazzled, unable to pursue any of them.

But freezing or defaulting to rigid control are not the only options we have!

Enter Wonder Intervention Experiments (WIEs).

These are deliberate, mini experiments designed to spark curiosity, play, and creative thinking.

They cultivate **wonder**.

Wonder is:

- Novelty
- Sensory stimulation
- Open-ended exploration

- Fun
- Insight
- Play
- Possibility
- Intuition
- Reflection
- Imagination

A sense of wonder helps you loosen the grip of control and cuts down on the overwhelming sense of too much to process at once. It's like walking through a vast and wondrous forest like a child. Exploring. Playing. Discovering.

You probably already know from experience that sometimes, the most astounding ideas occur when you are at rest and not expecting them. You might have a eureka moment in a dream, a surprising conversation, or simply while your mind is idling and doing nothing in particular.

This is where creativity lives. Importantly, **this is a place you *cannot* reach if you are anxious or overthinking.**

Creative intelligence only blooms when we let go of control and relax. An open, experimental mindset is a perfect anecdote to the tight, rigid mindset of overthinking. WIEs can take two forms:

1. Daily habits
2. Joyful diversions and disruptions

Let's take a closer look at how both forms can help you gently interrupt overthinking loops, loosen rigid control, and open up some space for fresh thinking.

Set a Micro-Habit That Sparks Curiosity

Let's start with the first one—tiny daily habits.

The key here is that you really do want to keep things *small*. Pick something you can do every day that makes a little breathing space for your brain. In this space, you want to feel the possibility of something new happening.

You're not making some grand overnight transformation. You're not assigning yourself a difficult goal, so you can evaluate whether you've succeeded or failed at the end of it. You're not launching a totally new lifestyle or committing to a whole new identity.

You're just curious.

You're just playing.

The daily WIE habit is not a conscious attempt at novelty or a performance; rather, it's just the *container* where something new might happen.

The fun thing about these is you can literally make them what you want. Some examples you could try for yourself:

- **Free writing in the morning for ten minutes.** No goal or agenda, no quota to fill, just put pen to paper and make sure you're writing something continuously for ten minutes' straight. What happens?
- **Sitting quietly.** Yes, just sitting quietly for a time. Not meditating, not visualizing. Not doing any kind of relaxation exercise. Just sitting and doing "nothing." Incidentally, if you've ever wondered why people have "shower thoughts" this is why—the shower is one of life's few screen-free places, where we can just be alone with our thoughts.
- **Doodle**. Take a few minutes to mess around with a pen or pencil. You're not performing for anyone, there's no score, and you can't do it right or wrong. Just gather data. Follow your nose (or your pen).

Do Something Creative That Has No Purpose

Now onto the second kind, joyful diversions—which are exactly what they sound like.

Imagine you are completely embroiled in a tricky, overwhelming problem.

- Your brain's threat-detection mechanisms are activated
- Your analytical mind is switched on and grinding away
- You're tempted to respond by overthinking and tightening up control somehow

Instead of speeding down this road of tension—hit the brakes. Just pause for a moment.

Imagine the current problem you're overthinking is a kind of quicksand—the more you panic and thrash around, the faster you sink. *So stop struggling.* More of the same is not going to help. Instead, you need a sudden perspective switch. You need a diversion. A distraction.

It may not feel like it at first, but your most reliable way out of the pit is to pivot and do something creative that has no purpose. Let go of linear, outcome-driven thinking, let go of logic and tunnel vision, and let go of your own fear and resistance.

Instead, do something "useless" that completely changes the channel in your brain.

- Bake or cook something
- Watch the birds
- Put an unusual outfit together
- Make a sketch
- Dance around the room to your favorite song
- Write a rude limerick
- Find a novel way to repurpose something you were going to throw out
- Make origami
- Play an ingenious prank on someone
- Go exploring in a part of the neighborhood you've never seen before
- Invent a new animal
- Mess around with clay
- Build something out of rocks
- Write a rap song with a friend
- Go on a walk and photograph all the stray cats you find

The activity can be anything you like—half the fun is imagining what you'd like it to be. The only "rule" is that it's low-stakes, sensory-rich, and creative. Make sure it's not connected in any way to the current problem you're overthinking. The sillier it is, the better—after all, there's no way to overthink something that isn't even trying to make sense!

Remind yourself that you don't need to be good, and that there isn't any specific outcome you're aiming for, or state you're trying to avoid. It's experimental. That means you aren't trying to *do* anything at all, but rather just be present and see what unfolds.

Your analytical mind may try to interrupt. Don't let it.

You're not wasting time. You're incubating.

You may find that your best insights and ideas come to you not when you're anxiously trying to hunt them out, but at precisely the moment you stop looking for them.

Imagine that—you can solve a problem by *under*thinking!

Go Outside and Track Something That Grows

Nature is not an overthinker, and she can teach you how to be more like her.

Nature doesn't rush, yet she gets everything done exactly on time.

Nature doesn't force anything. She allows things to grow and unfold at just the right pace.

Nature can be unpleasant and unpredictable. She can be cruel, strange, and fearsome, too. But one thing she never is? *Anxious*.

So, **use nature to help you disrupt the anxiety pattern.**

- Go for a color walk or similar
- Sit on your porch and observe
- Plant a seed and carefully track its growth over the days and weeks
- Notice how a particular area changes over the course of a day, month, or year
- Watch the behavior of birds, squirrels, or other animals
- Observe the movement of clouds, waves, or swaying trees

Your observations here are not idle or aimless. Remember to come with an open-ended and essentially *experimental* attitude. Perceive with intention. Have curious eyes. Listen like you mean it.

Let nature invite you into a slower, gentler pace, where a deeper and more grounded sense of wonder can grow.

You might be wrestling with an issue but one day take yourself outside to explore the many wonderful colors of fallen leaves. The tension and resistance leaves you, and your awareness fills with new ideas—ideas about graceful transition, about beauty in death, about richness and depth in unexpected places.

And suddenly, you have an aha moment about the issue you've been wrestling with. It's not that you were trying to solve this problem, It's just that nature has prompted you to see things a little differently. And that shift, that release, is what brings fresh insights.

DARE Method

"Stress is not what happens to us. It's our RESPONSE to what happens. And RESPONSE is something we can choose."

- **Maureen Killoran**

An overthinking problem is an anxiety problem.

Not every overthinker has a full-blown anxiety disorder, but that doesn't mean that anxiety isn't influencing their lives in smaller, everyday ways. For example:

- Procrastination
- Occasional physical symptoms like an upset stomach or headaches
- Insomnia
- Low mood
- Social anxiety
- Avoiding things
- Burning out
- Irritability
- Poor lifestyle choices, like binging, drinking, or other addictive behaviors
- Relationship difficulties
- Trouble making decisions

Though Barry McDonagh's book *Dare: The New Way to End Anxiety and Stop Panic Attacks* was written for those with diagnosed anxiety disorders, it contains some helpful tools for us overthinkers, too.

McDonagh begins with a surprising claim: **We can't turn anxiety off.**

That means that there's no point trying to escape or suppress our anxiety, and no point in judging ourselves when we utterly fail to do so. It's control again.

We feel out of control, we anxiously try to regain it, we fail, then we feel bad for failing.

Instead, stop the struggle entirely. Get out of the vicious cycle and realize that trying to escape anxiety only increases your fear, and reinforces the idea that you have something to be afraid of in the first place.

Instead, McDonagh's approach is to do something counterintuitive. This is captured in the acronym DARE:

1. Defuse
2. Accept and Allow
3. Run Toward
4. Engage

Overthinking is an expression of and response to anxiety. It's our brain's attempt to manage, predict, and control that anxiety.

But what if, instead, we just accepted anxiety as something normal? Something that couldn't actually hurt us?

Here's a paradox:

What happens to unacceptable feelings when you accept them?

What happens to a sense of unease when we are at peace with it?

Making friends with our feelings helps them to pass more easily. Going into anxious resistance or escape is ironically a way of holding onto and prolonging uncomfortable feelings. Whether we cling or resist, we are still trapped. The way out is to stop the war entirely: When we accept our fear, in time, it dissolves.

Let's say you have a new health complaint that has you fearful that something more serious is brewing. And so, you're anxious. We've already seen how overthinking is an attempt to manage uncertainty and vulnerability, but it's also a way to manage our own feelings of anxiety.

If we find our own fear unacceptable, then we may think, "Right, I need to do something so that I'm not so afraid anymore."

Let's say you go online to research—a common anxiety response to health concerns. You soon spiral. I don't have to tell you what happens next, right?

But let's rewind a little, to that point where you first notice the health complaint. What if you simply accepted that anxiety... and moved on? "I'm noticing I'm a little anxious right now. That's OK. It's uncomfortable, but it won't kill me."

You're not attaching to the anxiety nor are you desperately trying to escape it. You're just normalizing it. Just like that, much of its power drains away.

- No thinking "I'm going crazy"
- No need to fake it or pretend you're not anxious
- No desperate fix-it attempts or problem-solving missions
- No fear of your own thoughts or feelings
- No gaslighting yourself
- No shame
- No judgment

Just acceptance.

There's nothing for your brain to figure out or fix or fight against.

When you drop the need to judge, fix, or avoid, you actually discover a new way to reframe your experience—a more comfortable way.

It's making the shift from "What if a disaster happens?!" to "So what if a disaster happens?"

The spiral stops.

You rest.

Here's how to apply DARE and start making the switch in your own thinking:

Defuse the Thought with "So What?"
We've already explored the two most anxiety-provoking words in the English language: *what if.*

We've seen that much of its sting can be removed if we replace it with the more open, more accepting, *we'll see.*

DARE has some additional tips and tricks for disarming the "what if" mind bomb and they're called, appropriately, *defusing*.

Defuse = take the fuse off an explosive device.

When we defuse, we take something and make it less dangerous, less frightening.

How do we defuse a thought?

Not by arguing with it, avoiding it, or running away screaming from it. That only gives it more power, and makes it seem more dangerous. Instead, we knock its power out by simply being nonchalant about it.

It's those "so what?" vibes we're after.

The bomb is still there, but it no longer has its fuse. It's not such a big deal anymore. We neutralize all the emotional charge, so that there's nothing to be scared of.

Let's say I have a thought: "What if I mess up this interview and don't get the job?"

Feels bad. That's anxiety! Let's explore a few options:

- **Fight**: "Why am I like this? Worrying this way is unacceptable, I should have more confidence in myself. I hate being anxious!"

- **Control**: "I know, I can plan ahead. I can research other jobs. I can figure it out. Even if I stay up till 4am to do it…"
- **Agree**: "Yes, and what if I don't get this job or *any* job *ever* again? What if I lose everything and eventually die homeless and alone? What if…"

None of these are great options, and they can all quickly spiral into overthinking. Here's an option that helps you defuse instead:

"Ah well, so what. Even if I do mess up this interview, it won't be the first time it's happened, and probably not the last time either. I've navigated job changes in the past and I'll find a way through this time, too."

Here, you're not dismissing your fear, nor are you giving into it. You're just disarming it and taking it down a peg.

Anxiety comes and goes. So what?

Even if you have a full-blown panic attack and embarrass yourself in public—so what?

You'll have one, then it'll stop and you'll go on living. Anxiety never killed anyone.

Allow the Feeling Instead of Fighting It
Feel the anxiety; don't fight it.

Many of us are afraid to accept our feelings of anxiety because we believe that if we relinquish control, things will get out of hand. If we don't do something to fight and resist, then that somehow means we're agreeing to feel bad. Right?

But accepting how you feel is none of these things. It's simply recognizing the fact that anxiety works in strange ways—it's like a Chinese finger trap that tightens its grip on you the more you try to escape it.

Leaning into discomfort feels scary because we imagine that doing so will *increase* the negative feelings. But the opposite is usually true.

"I accept and allow this anxious feeling."

Note, this does ***not*** mean that:

- You agree with the feeling
- You want it to continue
- You like the feeling
- You think the feeling is fair or just
- You understand the feeling

It just means that you accurately perceive that this is in fact your reality. And that's a pretty neutral thing to do, after all.

In truth, it's anxious overthinking that increases negative experiences, not acceptance. There are two things going on:

- The primary sensation
- The secondary sensation—i.e., our emotional reactions to the primary sensation

What happens to anxiety when you're anxious to have it? Well, that's easy: It increases.

Acceptance dials down those secondary sensations. Acceptance helps us let go of the struggle.

The more you accept, the less power the anxiety holds.

YOU are the one who holds the real power.

Replace Escape with Approach
The R in DARE is for Run toward.

When we are anxious, we perceive neutral things as though they were threats. We even treat our own anxiety as a threat.

The only logical response to a threat?

Fight or flight.

In other words, go to war with the threat, run away from it—or both.

But these responses reinforce and confirm the appraisal of the situation as a threat in the first place.

For example, I'm going to a party tonight. Here's how my thought process goes:

1. My perception: party = danger
2. The result of my perception: I'm anxious
3. My secondary perception: anxiety = danger
4. The result of my secondary perception: I'm *more* anxious
5. I'm overthinking now.
6. I'm *really* overthinking now
7. Ok, screw it, I'm not going
8. [sweet relief]
9. Therefore, party = danger, but not going to party = relief
10. Conclusion: Avoidance is useful, parties really are scary, and staying home is the best choice for me.

I'm sure you can see what's gone wrong here. But how do we break the cycle?

Replace escape with approach. Like so:

1. My perception: party = danger

2. The result of my perception: I'm anxious
3. My secondary perception: anxiety = danger
4. The result of my secondary perception: I'm *more* anxious
5. I'm overthinking now.
6. **Screw it, I'm going anyway**
7. I go. Oh hey, this isn't so bad
8. I think I'm having a nice time
9. Correction: party = sometimes fun
10. Conclusion: Anxiety doesn't necessarily mean anything. Parties aren't dangerous.

The difference is that we approach our fear, rather than avoid it.

The same thing applies when we approach our own anxiety. I can fully acknowledge that I'm feeling anxious about the party... and go anyway.

Another way to think of it: *Approach* is a kind of mini experiment.

Anxiety only offers you foregone conclusions and definitive statements: ***This is scary.***

But curiosity and experimentation pose an open question: ***What is this?***

Reframe the Sensation as Excitement
The final step is the trickiest one.

Anxiety is nervous system arousal. It's almost physiologically identical to the sensation of excitement—it's only our perception that tells us which is which.

We can use this to our advantage.

The next time you feel anxious—your heart is racing, your muscles are tightening—try say to yourself **"These sensations are excitement."**

- What if your body isn't fearful, it's just preparing to act?
- What if you're not anxious, you're just alert and engaged?
- What if there isn't anything to fight against or overthink, just a sensation to experience and ride out like any other?

Then you feel what you're feeling without interpreting it as fear.

Caveat: The DARE method is for use when you already know your fear is not based in reality... but you're anxious anyway. While 90% of rumination falls into this category, please use discretion and avoid using defusion, acceptance, approach, and reframing to encourage yourself to stay in a genuinely unsafe situation.

3-Second Anxiety Relief

"The moment is not found by seeking it, but by ceasing to escape from it."

- **James Pierce**

Let's imagine you're sitting somewhere quietly on a sofa, reading an interesting book about anxiety management. You're drinking a nice cup of coffee and the birds outside are chittering away pleasantly. It's a lazy, comfy Sunday afternoon.

The book is telling you all about meditation, about helpful breathing exercises, and about reframing your core beliefs by using a pretty journal to write down and gently unpick your negative thought patterns. It's talking about self-care and pacing and how to be mindful.

"Sounds nice!" you think. "I should try some of these things for myself next time I'm feeling anxious."

Fast forward a few days and *boom*, you're having a minor panic attack.

You're spiraling, and fast.

Your heart is pounding, your mouth is dry, and you feel like your head's going to explode.

What about the breathing exercise and the self-care and the pretty thought journal?

Yeah right!

The truth is that by the time you are aware of being anxious:

- Your HPA axis (the three-gland network of hypothalamus, pituitary, and adrenals) is already fully active
- Your sympathetic nervous system is already triggered
- You are already firmly in fight-or-flight
- You're already outside your window of tolerance

In short: *You are already in survival mode.*

A story of two brain parts

Imagine your brain is a medieval castle.

Imagine that in your brain castle there is a monkish scribe sitting in the high tower, carefully counting up the castle's gold, keeping court records, organizing the peasant's work schedules, and planning out battle strategy.

There's also a watchman on the wall. He closely monitors the environment for marauding troops and other threats, and raises the alarm if he thinks the castle is under attack. His alarm is deafening and terrifying and impossible to ignore—he shouts and screams and bangs gongs and blows trumpets.

Once the watchman raises that noisy alarm, the scribe has to abandon all his efforts and temporarily shut down his workstation so he can respond to the watchman's alarm.

The thing is, so long as the watchman is raising the alarm, the scribe can't sit down and do his slower, more precise work. It's only once the watchman calms down again and goes back to his station that the scribe can continue on with his important business.

In this story, the watchman is the **amygdala**.

His work is valuable for survival, so he has to act fast and ask questions later, but that means he sometimes makes mistakes.

Every time your brain detects a threat, it triggers a cascade of neurochemical and hormonal stress responses in the body.

While all this is happening, though, the scribe—who is the **prefrontal cortex** in the brain—can't do his job properly. He can't think, plan ahead, be creative, or analyze logically.

When you are panicking, it is *physiologically impossible* to activate the parts of your brain that are associated with rational thought, logic, and sound decision making. Read that again: It's a physiological impossibility.

Only the scribe or the watchman can be active at any one point—never both at the same time.

So how do we get around this?

When the watchman raises a false alarm, how do we quickly get him to calm down and go back to his post?

- Meditation?
- Journaling?
- Self-love affirmations?
- CBT techniques?
- Pacing?
- Breathing exercises?
- Stress management techniques?

You can see the problem: All of these approaches can work, but they require a degree of reasoning that is simply not available to us when we're in the middle of an anxiety spiral. It's easy to see what a good idea they are when we're calm... but when we're not calm, all these good ideas fly right out the window.

Instead, in an emergency, we need something **simple** and **fast**.

The 3-second anxiety relief technique we'll discuss below is one such alternative.

It doesn't require reasoning or a clear head—it just requires re-connecting to your immediate, present reality for three consecutive seconds. That's it.

This trick is great for use during full-blown panic attacks, but you can also use it any time you feel:

- Overwhelmed
- Uncertain
- Fearful
- Stressed out
- Disoriented
- Out of control
- Chaotic
- Disorganized

You anchor back to reality using your **physical senses**, **language,** and **time awareness** to reactivate your prefrontal cortex and get the amygdala to calm down.

The method puts your brain into a kind of "reality check" mode—perhaps even more effectively and reliably than something like meditation or breathing exercises.

How does it work?

Snap Your Fingers Twice
It may sound strange, but the first step is this: Snap your fingers together, twice.

It's a tiny gesture, but a deliberate one. It's the physicality of this action that activates your sensory cortex and brings you out of your anxiety loop and back into the here-and-now. Snapping fingers serve as a kind of reset button and is a cultural shorthand for, "Hey, look here!"

You are telling your brain to redirect:

- From chaotic to intentional
- From mental to sensory
- From internal to external

And in those split seconds it takes you to snap your fingers twice and take notice of yourself doing it, you have already begun to interrupt the anxiety momentum that was steamrolling you just a moment ago.

Verbally State Your Current Coordinates

Now, out loud, verbally make a statement:

"[Your name] is at [place] on [day, date, or time]."

You can play around with the order if you like.

Examples:

- "Jordan is in her kitchen on Friday, August 9."
- "I'm in my office. It's 4:12 p.m. It's Monday."
- "Natasha. In the car. Tuesday afternoon."

These elements—time, person, and place—are all external, objective facts. They're all verifiable as part of actual reality. That might not seem like much of an achievement, but when you're in an anxiety storm, it may have been a while since your last encounter with reality!

Objective facts in the concreteness of time and place are like a port in that storm. When you anchor in them, you shift your attention just long enough to stop spiraling.

Identify Three Textures You Physically Feel
Once you've spoken out loud, anchor yourself further to the present moment by identifying distinct physical textures or sensations in your immediate environment.

- "The denim seam against my leg feels stiff and kind of rough."
- "The breeze from the air conditioner feels slightly ticklish against my skin."
- "The smooth surface of this notebook feels faintly squeaky, and a little cold under my fingertips."

The amygdala watchman is ultra-sensitive, and ready to interpret any tiny thing as a sign of threat. When you re-anchor in your senses, however, you give yourself a chance to update and adjust your perception of this threat.

Your head may be in a whirl, but have you noticed that here in your car, everything's completely chill and quiet?

That there is nothing much of anything going on, and that you're perfectly safe?

The car upholstery feels warm underneath you, and you can see that the golden sun has made visible the faint dust motes in the air that are falling very, very slowly downward, like snowflakes...

Your head has conjured up a vivid horror film for you... but have you noticed that *outside* your head, there are four little coins sitting in the cup holder over there? And that one of the coins is a copper one with beautiful turquoise tarnishing on one side? Have you ever noticed the subtle texture of the plastic on this dial over here?

You are here, now. And you are safe.

The tangible world is almost never as scary as the world we imagine in our minds.

Specificity is always more manageable than a vague, shapeless worry, which can technically be of infinite proportions.

Of course, it can be difficult to pull yourself out of the horror movie and back into reality, even for just a moment. But the good news is that you only have to do it for a moment for it to work. Give yourself just three seconds.

1. Snap your fingers
2. Speak out loud to yourself, nice and clearly
    a. Say your name
    b. Where you are
    c. What time it is

3. Then anchor yourself in your senses

That's all it takes.

The 3-Second Trick in Action
At a job interview

You're waiting in the reception area. You steal a few moments in the washroom before the meeting. You snap your fingers twice and say to your reflection in the mirror:

"You're Tina Mackey, you're at your job interview on Park Road, and it's 9:55 am on June 8th."

Then you have a look around the washroom and count the number of speckled black tiles that are along the perimeter of the walls.

At a funeral

You're overwhelmed and emotional. You're panicking, worried that you're going to do or say something you'll regret. You step outside for a moment, and snap your fingers. You're here. You're now.

"I'm Nick and I'm at St. Mary's and it's Saturday morning."

You can hear distant chatter inside the church. You run your fingers up the front of your shirt, then down again, tracing a little route around the buttons. You notice that each button has something printed on it, but you can't see what. You examine the orientation of this word on each of the buttons, and compare how each of them has been sewn on a little differently…

In just a few minutes, you feel on top of things again.

At the doctor

You're terrified of needles. There's a doctor here, and he's got a giant needle with your name on it. You cannot snap your fingers or speak aloud in quite the same way, since you're self-conscious about the doctor, so instead you say to him,

"You've got such an interesting chart on the wall there… that's the inner ear, right? *Malleus, incus, stapes*… hammer, anvil, stirrup…"

You look carefully at the crumpled texture of the corner of that poster, of how the color has faded ever so slightly to yellow on the very furthest edges…

You don't notice the needle go in.

When experiencing late night existential dread

You're in bed and you should be sleeping, but you're not.

What's the point of this life? Where's it all *going*? What's actually wrong with you? Why does your back hurt, anyway? You've wasted your life and it's too late now...

Stop.

You snap your fingers.

"My name is Sam. I'm at 67 Corban Avenue, in my house, in bed. It's 3am on September 12th. It's a Wednesday."

Then you run your fingers over the ridged pattern of your cotton bedspread. Done slowly enough, you can even feel the ridges of your own fingerprints against one another.

You take a deep breath. You're safe.

The watchman can go back to his wall. Let the scribe go back to being in charge. And he says: *Everything's fine. Let's go to sleep.*

Choose Again Method

"The greatest weapon against stress is our ability to choose one thought over another."

- **William James**

What actually causes thoughts to spiral?

It's like a tiny little puff of cloud that you first notice far away on the horizon. But the more you look at it, the more it seems to grows bigger and darker, coming closer and closer, until suddenly you're *in* that dark cloud and it's surrounding you on all sides. Before you know it, there's a full-blown storm— thunder, lightning, hail.

How did that tiny puff of cloud turn into *this*?

- Maybe you started out a little on edge because of the size of your to-do list, but landed with a whirlwind of dark and negative feelings about your entire self-worth as a human being…
- Maybe you started out focusing on a tiny imperfection in your appearance, but in no time you stirred up a wave of toxic feelings about being abandoned, forgotten, or unloved…

- Maybe you started out hearing a little constructive feedback about your work, but now you're stuck in a loop of negative thinking that's completely hijacking your clarity and happiness…

What's going on? How does the small thing turn into the Big Thing?

You're not lazy, you're not crazy, and you're not broken.

But you are stuck. And the reason you're stuck is that you've allowed one negative thought to string onto another, and another, again and again, like the plastic monkeys in a Barrel of Monkeys game.

A negative thought spiral typically looks like this:

1. You have a negative thought.
2. Your brain readily takes your word for it. If you're thinking it, it must be true, right?
3. You feel bad because of that thought.
4. Because you feel bad, you think another negative thought.
5. You feel even worse because of *that* thought.
6. And on and on…

It's a **self-amplifying feedback loop.**

Each negative thought leads smoothly onto the next because at no point do you stop and say, "Hang on, this isn't right. I don't *want* to think this." Instead, negativity fuels more negativity, and before you know it, you're spiraling.

Self-help author Gabby Bernstein has a simple three-step process she calls the Choose Again Method, which acts like a kind of circuit breaker for runaway thought spirals. It's a way to extinguish that little puff of cloud before it turns into a storm.

You interrupt your own mental noise and open up a little pocket of **intentionality**, in other words, recognizing that **you get to choose your thoughts**.

It's like this: If you chose *this* thought, and *this* thought doesn't feel good, then guess what? You can *choose again.*

We're not talking about

- Wishful thinking
- Toxic positivity
- Repressing true feelings
- Ignoring stress

Instead, it's about calmly reclaiming your own mental space and returning to clarity.

Go back and look at step 2 of the negative thought spiral:

> *Your brain readily takes your word for it. If you're thinking it, it must be true, right?*

This is the key. Your brain accepts and believes whatever you tell it to. If you think it's important to focus on, then your brain thinks it's real. That means if you've been feeding yourself a steady diet of thoughts along the lines of...

- I'll never do enough, have enough, or be enough
- There's something wrong with me
- I must perform perfectly to be accepted by others

...and so on, then your brain will simply take all this to be fact.

Repetition becomes reality.

At any time, however, you can stop.

You can choose again.

Let's take a look at how.

Notice the Thought
As with so many things, the first step is to find awareness. You need to know that you

are, in fact, having a negative thought if you hope to move on from it.

- "I'm falling behind."
- "I can't handle this."
- "Everything's just a big mess."

OK, there it is. A negative thought. Now just pause. There's no need to judge this thought, put yourself down for having it, or go to war with it in any way.

All you need to do is be aware, and put a neutral, accurate label on the sensation.

- "I'm feeling **uncertain** about my next steps right now."
- "I'm **overwhelmed** and have too many open tasks."
- "I'm feeling **discouraged** by this situation."

Forgive the Thought
This next step is important.

Once you've become aware of a thought, deliberately loosen your grip on it. Soften yourself. Choose to let go and release, rather than continue to hold on.

You're not a bad person for having this experience, it's not a mistake and, importantly, *you don't have to keep having it.*

Let it go with compassion.

In Bernstein's process, now is the time to say, **"I forgive myself for having this thought. Thank you for showing me what I don't want, so I can focus on what I do."**

That means that if you feel uncertain, overwhelmed, or discouraged, for example, that's OK. There's no need to argue, fix, judge, or resist. Just *accept*... and move on.

Let go of struggle and resistance, and disidentify from the thought. It's not yours anymore, and you don't have to carry it. When you do, you make space for something else—something better.

Choose Again
The final step is to ask yourself, **"What's the next best feeling or thought I can reach for now?"**

Importantly, this doesn't have to be a total, dramatic transformation. It just needs to be *better*.

It needs to be a true and empowering step forward, in the opposite direction that you were being nudged in by the negative thought.

- "I'm falling behind," becomes "I don't have to perform at the same intensity every day. Today's been a slower day, and that's OK."
- "I can't handle this," becomes "This is challenging. I've handled challenging things before, and I'll find a way through this time, too."
- "Everything's just a big mess," becomes "I don't have to understand everything all at once. There are a few things I can do right now that make sense and feel good."

You might write these things down, or simply say them out loud to yourself.

When you choose a different thought, you empower yourself to choose a different action. A new world of possibility opens up.

A few tips:

- There's no point getting upset with yourself for being upset. Instead of beating yourself up for getting lost in an anxiety spiral, celebrate the fact that you found a way out.
- Use your negative feelings as fuel to move onto something better. What

messages are these feelings sharing with you? What can they teach you?
- No matter how bad you feel or how far into anxiety you slip, remind yourself that you *always* have the option, at any time, to stop and choose again.
- When you're feeling especially low or anxious, it's usually not easy to pull yourself into a more positive mindset. So just take baby steps. You don't have to launch yourself into immediate happiness—just into a state of a little less negativity.
- You can run through this process multiple times a day, finetuning your way out of negative loops and patterns, and into feeling better and more in control.

Think of it as negative thought "cloud bursting."

Bank Of Good Thoughts

"The worst of our faults is our interest in other people's faults."

- **Ali ibn Abi Talib**

Tamara adores her fiancé.

She is going to marry him in 6 months' time.

She's in love, she's happy, and she's looking forward to the wedding.

And yet…

One day, Tamara is watching TV with her fiancé when she notices a weird little thing he does with his top lip when he laughs. How had she never noticed it before?

Soon, it's the only thing she *can* notice.

She doesn't like it one bit. It's weird and off putting, and the more she watches him, the worse it seems.

Then, she notices herself noticing. She notices her own irritation.

"Oh my God, what is going on with me? How can I think such awful thoughts about the man I love?"

Now *this* worries her. She notices herself being worried—does the worry itself signal something?

But Tamara can't stop. In no time, she's second-guessing *everything*. Does she really love him? Really? Is he actually completely wrong for her in every single way? Is she about to make the biggest mistake of her life in marrying him?!

Relationship overthinking can have many complicated causes, but its most basic underlying mechanism is this: **A simple moment of tension is allowed to snowball out of control**.

- Tamara makes a tiny observation
- She perceives it as a threat/problem
- In reactive/survival/fight-or-flight/resistance/judgment mode, she gets to work on escaping or going to war with this "problem"
- She feels a wave of secondary negative emotions as a result
- She judges these emotions, too
- In reactive/survival/fight-or-flight/resistance/judgment mode, she gets to work on escaping or going to war with *herself,* as she is now also a problem

- And before she knows it, she's stuck in an overthinking loop, questioning everything

Importantly, the spiral of judgment, shame, and doubt is launched precisely because of her negative reaction to the original trigger. Not the trigger itself. In other words, the problem is 0.1% what her fiancé has done, and 99.9% what she has made of it.

Mike Massimino is a NASA astronaut and ex-engineering professor at Columbia University. He's learned a few things about leadership strategy and managing teams in high-pressure environments.

His "Bank of Good Thoughts" method was originally devised as a management tool and a way to approach conflict and misunderstanding in the workplace. However, the technique is perfectly suited to Tamara and those of us who struggle with **relationship overthinking.**

- Have you ever caught yourself quietly tallying up a list of faults and flaws of the people closest to you?
- Do you sometimes struggle with doubt, jealousy, paranoia, insecurity, or a feeling that your relationship is

always at the mercy of a threat you can't quite put into words?
- Do you spend a lot of time after social events or conversations ruminating over what people *really* meant?
- Do you often second-guess yourself or them, as though the relationship is always on the brink of ending?
- Do you often find yourself comparing your relationships to other peoples', or agonizing over what's "normal"?

If so, relationship overthinking may be an issue for you.

Why do some of us make relationships the target of so much anxious rumination?

We may be trapped in fear loops and thought patterns that were ingrained during childhood, where our caregivers were unreliable or abusive. Hypervigilance and a nervous system that is overly sensitive to threat detection may be the result of early trauma and loss, or negative relationship experiences in adulthood.

Whatever the cause, relationship overthinking often expresses itself as

- negative automatic assumptions about other people

- continually jumping to the worst-case scenario
- doubt, uncertainty, and restlessness
- a fear of abandonment

How do we change?

IMPORTANT: The shift we make is a shift in *perception*.

We cannot change Tamara's fiancé and who he really is as a person. He really *does* do that weird thing with his lip while watching TV.

Our goal is not perfection or control over others.

Our goal is to choose to see people as more than their faults.

The Bank of Good Thoughts technique is a way for us to acknowledge that people aren't perfect, we're not perfect, and our relationships are not perfect—but without turning this normal imperfection into a full-blown, catastrophic threat.

Make Regular Deposits
It's easy to zoom in on someone's annoying little faults and bad habits.

But let's reframe:

- What do you *like* about them?

- What good things do they bring to the table that no other person can?
- What is an admirable trait in them that you value?
- What useful things can you learn from them?
- What good experiences have you already shared together?

Try to make regular small "deposits" into your Good Thoughts bank account so that when other people eventually slip up or do something to annoy you (which they will!) then your store of goodwill for them will be so heavily in credit that it doesn't matter.

You can make your deposits in a notebook or simply store them up in your memory.

- *My fiancé is a smart, funny guy*
- *My fiancé is the only one in the world who knows how to make lasagna the way I like it*
- *My fiancé and I have been through six happy years together*
- *My fiancé is often kind and understanding when I'm in a bad mood*
- *My fiancé has taught me so much about hard work and perseverance*

Against all this, his weird little quirk doesn't seem so bad, right?

If you maintain a baseline feeling of gratitude, admiration, and appreciation for someone, then you'll approach any minor annoyance with far more tact, grace, and accommodation.

Importantly, you won't be tempted to overthink. Rather, you'll skim over the snag and instead focus on why you're in this relationship in the first place.

- Just take a breath.
- Turn your threat detection way down.
- Then pivot your thoughts to everything you have to be thankful for.

Your storehouse of kind thoughts is a healthy counterbalance to the negative tunnel vision that anxiety will trap you in. In fight-or-flight mode, the mind is obsessed with identifying and focusing on the threat, the flaw, and the problem… even if there isn't one!

Gently relax out of this frame by reminding yourself that, **on balance, this person you are in a relationship with is a friend, not a foe.**

Withdraw Before You React

Overthinking is mental torture for the one experiencing it, but what happens when this inner turmoil spills into the outside world?

In other words, what if Tamara gets so annoyed with her fiancé that later, after she's stewed over her anxious thoughts for hours, she suddenly snaps at him. Understandably, he'd feel like this outburst came "from nowhere."

Tamara may be anxious and upset but unsure why.

"What if we're just too different, you and I?"

"It's not supposed to be this hard. This is meant to be the honeymoon period!"

"You don't understand me…"

If Tamara's fiancé happens to be a relationship overthinker himself, this is bad news. Her words will act as a trigger for him, and soon he too will be in reactive fight-or-flight mode, focusing in on the "problem."

Here's an alternative: When you notice yourself annoyed by someone, or when there's a moment of miscommunication, conflict, or bad feeling, just pause.

Choose to **respond rather than react**.

- Don't spiral into assumptions
- Don't tell stories about other people's motivations
- Don't zoom in on hurt and make it bigger
- Don't connect what's happening now to things from the past

Instead, dial down the intensity.

Come out of judgment, fear, and threat.

Withdraw internally and go to your Bank of Good Thoughts and draw out some goodwill.

"OK, so he has an annoying habit. He's gotten a little defensive about it, which is understandable. But this is also the man who just yesterday got up early to make me a fancy coffee to enjoy in bed. I love him."

Redirect with Respect
When your mind is anxious, it's because it's responding to a perceived threat.

In survival mode, you experience narrowed tunnel vision, and you stop seeing the bigger picture. You also stop seeing the other person. All that matters is your own protection, at any cost.

Ironically, this may make you behave in callous and insensitive ways.

Instead, try to address any difficult situations from a place of clarity and compasison, rather than defensiveness.

That means consciously choosing to:

- Relax
- Reframe
- Redirect

Defensiveness doesn't help—it only invites more defensiveness from others.

Instead, choose the clarity that comes from the middle path: **Acknowledge potential issues and problems while still honoring the relationship in which they arise.**

It may be that the thing bothering Tamara is not a harmless personal quirk, but a genuine grievance. Imagine, for example, that she's noticed a growing habit of him promising to do some task then failing to keep his word.

In this case, Tamara can pause, withdraw to remind herself of her fiancé's good qualities, then approach with an intention to prompt, respectful, and productive conversation.

Overthinking can too often lead to overreacting, overanalyzing, over-explaininig, over-justifying, over-attacking, over-discussing, over-defending…

Instead,

- Make sure you're fully relaxed
- Come comfortably into your window of tolerance
- Dial down your nervous system's threat detection. Tell yourself:
    - there is no threat
    - this is a conversation, not a confrontation
    - this person is a friend, not an enemy

Once you're in *that* frame of mind, then approach:

"Hey, I know that you're a hard worker and that you care about the life we're building together. I've noticed you haven't done that task you promised you'd do. Can we figure this out together?"

No blame, no shame, and no overthinking.

Just open, respectful communication.

Four-Step Method

"We cannot solve our problems with the same thinking we used when we created them."

- **Albert Einstein**

Unless you've been living under a rock for the last ten years, you're probably aware of mindfulness and meditation. While there *is* plenty of good evidence to support these approaches, it's also true that certain forms of meditation can exacerbate and aggravate overthinking.

Jeffrey Schwartz is a research psychiatrist and author of *You Are Not Your Brain*, and he has created a four-step *applied* mindfulness approach that can work wonders for ruminators. The four steps are simple:

1. **Relabel**
2. **Reframe**
3. **Refocus**
4. **Revaluc**

Firstly, some normalizing:

Everyone experiences cognitive distortions at times.

Everyone has a brain that gets things wrong occasionally.

Everyone feels overwhelmed now and then.

None of this means that we have an anxiety disorder, or something is wrong or bad with us. Schwartz's method was originally intended for OCD patients, but can be used by anyone who wants to learn to observe, shift, and retrain their unhelpful thought patterns.

According to Schwartz, the more we practice and apply these four steps, the more we cultivate our inner "wise advocate"—that clear, calm inner voice that helps us react with conscious intention, and not with reactive fear.

Before we jump into the four steps, let's consider a foundational idea:

The "overthinking voice" is not the same as our real voice.

It's important that you clearly discern the difference.

Learn to recognize when it's your fear talking, not you.

Try to personify this voice, maybe even giving it a name and identity. When you notice an anxious and irrational thought pop up, create some psychological distance by saying:

"Oh, it's you! You're that familiar old thought pattern... I'm going to call you *The Accuser* because that's what you do!"

Any time you hear that voice, consciously tell yourself: "This is just The Accuser talking again, not me."

See this voice for what it is: Background noise. The mental equivalent of an annoying fly. Something that lacks reality and authority.

Relabel the Thought

Your job is to try and catch thought spirals before they begin.

Your job is *not* to:

- Judge
- Suppress
- Negotiate
- Plead
- Entertain
- Agree or disagree
- Justify
- Analyze
- Shame

Instead, simply label the phenomenon. Ignore the content for now.

"I'm overthinking."

"This is a fear-based thought."

"My brain is caught on that same old loop again."

When you label, you create breathing space and psychological distance. You remind yourself that **you are not your thoughts.**

Anxiety tells us that thoughts are

- Important
- True
- Commands we have to follow
- Permanent
- Urgent
- Personal
- Pervasive
- Unavoidable

But none of this is necessarily true. A thought is just a thought—it's just an event in the mind. Electrochemical activity in the synapses. It's here, and then it's gone.

A thought is not automatically true, important, or urgent.

A thought isn't a command we have to obey—in fact, we don't have to react to it at all.

A thought doesn't say anything meaningful about who we are as people.

When you label your thoughts, you identify it as what it is: a temporary mental event. That's all.

Reframe the Meaning
Once you label a thought, you can set it off to the side at some distance, so you can have a proper look at it.

We can be fused or de-fused from our thoughts.

Fused with the thought – the thought is close to us—so close we assume it's reality. We cannot see it or ourselves properly. We are inside the thought. We *are* the thought.

De-fused from the thought – the thought is a little removed from us; it's now a thought as such, not reality itself. We can see it more clearly for what it is. We *are not* this thought.

Once there's some distance, consider your thought with fresh eyes. Remember that the meaning we find in thoughts comes from *us*. Take a good look and see if some of the meaning you see is actually coming from cognitive distortions.

Cognitive distortions add meaning to reality that isn't actually there. Here are some examples of common cognitive distortions:

- All or nothing, black and white thinking – "She didn't reply; so obviously she hates me."
- Emotional reasoning – "I feel insulted, so someone must have insulted me."
- Catastrophizing – "This will ruin my entire life."
- Taking things personally – "I'm to blame if he's unhappy."
- Mind reading – "She didn't say anything but I know she hates it."
- Overgeneralization – "Life isn't fair!"
- "Should" statements – "I shouldn't find this as hard as I do."
- Discounting the positive – "Everyone passes that exam, it doesn't mean anything."
- Magnifying or minimizing – "His feedback was a total attack on me as a person."

Instead, **shift to calm, reflective thinking**: "I'm feeling anxious, but that doesn't mean the situation is actually dangerous."

"I've had a thought, but that doesn't automatically mean the thought is true, accurate, or helpful."

Invite your wise advocate to weigh in, not your knee-jerk fear.

Instead of thinking from inside your fear, find calm and clarity first, *then* explore alternative explanations and interpretations.

What are your values? What are your goals? What's the bigger picture here? You can only align with those things if you can come out of reactive fear, and de-fuse from anxious thoughts.

Refocus Your Attention

Once you've named the thought, created a little distance and asked your wiser self to weigh in on some alternative meanings, then you are free to start redirecting your energy and attention elsewhere.

This is not dissimilar to the "Choose Again" technique discussed earlier:

1. Notice the thought
2. Forgive the thought
3. Choose again

When we choose another thought, we are consciously choosing to redirect energy and attention without force, shame, or blame.

This is not rumination. It's choosing small, purposeful actions that kick you out of your mental inertia and thought traps.

What should you refocus on? Well, that's up to you!

Check in with your inner wise advocate to see what you need most in this moment:

- To ground yourself in your senses? Try a walk outside, some exercise, or stretches.
- To take conscious action? Make a first move on a task or get started on a project.
- To soothe and relax yourself? Chat with a friend, have a nap, or enjoy a hobby.
- To anchor in your purpose again? Help someone, journal, reach out to a loved one, or remind yourself of your goals and values.
- To get out of a mental rut? Switch tasks and do something completely different. Try a Wonder Invention Experiment or a color walk.

IMPORTANT: You are not trying to escape the anxiety. You are not denying or repressing it. You are **consciously and deliberately choosing to redirect your attention**. Big difference!

It almost doesn't matter what you re-direct to; what's important is that you shift out of the loop and into real, constructive, forward momentum again.

Revalue the Thought

If these steps seem a little labored and unnatural, they shouldn't—you have probably gone through some version of every one of these steps in your own mind already. If you are firmly within your window of tolerance, calm, conscious, and in control, then these adjustments will come more naturally.

If you're an overthinker, it's your negative thought patterns that are automatic. The good news is that the process can be reversed: you can approach life with a positive, productive interpretation locked and loaded, so that your kneejerk reaction is calm, composed, wise, and adaptive.

What would life look like if your default state was compassionate, grounded, and

strongly connected to what really mattered?

The truth is, we just give too much weight to the tired old thought patterns that keep us stuck.

- We put too much faith in them.
- We give them too much airtime.
- We make them matter more than they need to.

Instead, learn to revalue thoughts. Not every thought that pops into your mind with urgency really is urgent. Stop taking everything you think at face value. Stop agreeing to let your nervous system get hijacked by what essentially amounts to rumors and stories.

Remember Tamara from the previous chapter?

In Tamara's anxiety, she thought that her thoughts about her fiancé were very, very important indeed. They were a sign of trouble, proof that something was wrong, and a serious warning sign.

"If I'm so bothered but such a tiny thing he does, doesn't that mean that he can't be right for me?"

Actually, **no**. It doesn't mean that!

Tamara's not mad—she correctly identified a slightly annoying habit in her fiancé, and was, well, slightly annoyed by it. But what does that annoyance *mean*?

Take the time to make sure that the best part of you is making this evaluation, not the most frightened and anxious part.

"Gosh, he does a weird thing with his lip, I've never noticed that before. Not attractive! Oh well, I love him anyway."

The thought is there, just as it always was. It's just that Tamara is no longer acting like it's the most significant piece of information that has come to her all week. It's just a thought. It's no big deal. People who love each other sometimes find one another annoying. Totally normal and unremarkable!

What's changed here is not the thought itself, nor even its meaning. What's changed is the *weight* Tamara gives it.

See the thought. See the meaning you've given it. Then choose not to agree that it's of any consequence.

The Anxiety-Curiosity Switch

"Curiosity will conquer fear even more than bravery will."

- **James Stephens**

Imagine a little child, let's say two years old.

They're with their mom in a new environment, a playroom they've never seen before.

You watch their behavior closely. When they feel safe and relaxed, you see that they happily leave their mother's side and start exploring the room. They investigate everything, play, and engage with the other kids… all while keeping an eye on mom.

If something unexpected happens, though, they run back to mom and cling to her. The exploration ends. The play stops. Socializing is over.

Though this behavior is obvious in very young children, the truth is that the same thing happens to us adults.

Have you ever sat down to a creative task and felt yourself completely frozen and shut down? You may have called it "writer's block," but its real name? **Anxiety**.

Have you ever found that the moment someone starts to watch you do something, you can't do it anymore? It's **anxiety**.

Have you ever gotten stuck tweaking and refining a project, unable to stop and move on? It's not "perfectionism," it's plain old **anxiety**.

And the anxiety we feel in these situations is no different to the anxiety felt by the two-year-old.

The two-year-old cannot explore and play when they're afraid any more than you can do your creative task when *you're* feeling afraid. Your anxiety may show up as exhaustion, disinterest, irritation, boredom, despair, or a numb sense of being on autopilot. But nevertheless, it's anxiety, and it's coloring everything you do, think, and feel.

Curiosity mode

- It's about exploring, playing, creating, socializing, inventing, enjoying
- It feels flowy, joyful, and fun
- We open up
- We approach
- We ask open questions

- We are outside of problems, trying to solve them
- We expand or grow
- We become good at spotting possibilities and opportunities

Anxiety mode

- It's about clinging, avoiding, escaping, hiding, protecting, defending, cowering, detecting threats and surviving them
- It feels flat, tense, and urgent
- We close ourselves off
- We retreat or withdraw
- We make closed statements
- We are inside of problems, at their mercy
- We shrink or contract
- We become good at spotting flaws and problems

The curious thing is that both mental states—anxiety and curiosity—occupy the same networks in the brain (Hilmerich et.al., 2024, "Anxiety and curiosity in hierarchical models of neural emotion processing – A mini review").

What does this mean? Anxiety and curiosity are mutually exclusive: If we're

curious we can't be anxious, and if we're anxious we can't be curious.

It's a question of framing.

When we encounter a new situation, our main focus is going to be on the unpredictability and novelty of that situation. But is that a good or bad thing? Consider the two ways you might say the following:

"What's this?"

With fear and apprehension, we approach the unknown thinking:

- "What might go wrong?"
- "Where is the danger?"
- "How can I avoid it?"

In other words, anxiety = reactive, shut down.

With calm and confident curiosity, however, we can approach the unknown in a different way:

- "What might I discover?"
- "What's here for me?"
- "How can I get involved in what's happening here?"

It's the difference between walking through a garden during an Easter egg hunt and excitedly expecting something fun to appear vs. walking through a war zone, expecting landmines.

We can use the mutual exclusivity of curiosity and anxiety to our own advantage. Here's how.

Catch Yourself in the "Fix It" Loop

Few of us experience genuine threats to our survival day to day. That said, it's difficult to stay in an open, exploratory frame of mind. How are you going to feel "curious" and open when you're arguing with your partner, in a conflict with your child, or navigating an uncomfortable dispute with a colleague?

We've already touched on relationship overthinking, and how activating old learned fear responses can damage connections over time.

We stop responding to the person in front of us, and start reacting in automatic, kneejerk ways.

We make assumptions.

We jump to conclusions.

We get lost in guesswork and mindreading.

The result? The connection dulls and grows numb. Predictable.

The next time you're in a conversation with someone you care about, pause and become aware of yourself. Before you speak, ask yourself,

"Am I reacting from a place of anxiety or curiosity?"

Ask yourself if you are tempted to

- Solve
- Manage
- Control
- Fix
- Steer
- Teach

If so, you might launch into some unsolicited advice or be too ready to take responsibility for what you believe is unfolding.

Instead, just pause. Take a breath. Anxiety is urgent, but curiosity is in no rush.

Listen to understand, rather than to respond.

Ask Questions That Invite Surprise

Anxiety doesn't ask questions—it already knows how things are (bad, probably) and it doesn't need to learn anything new.

Without curiosity, we fall into predictable rote behavior patterns with people, and we forget that they're *not us* and that we don't automatically know what they think, what they feel, what they're going to do, or what they care about.

Because we're not curious, we don't ever allow ourselves to be *surprised* by others.

Sadly, this can happen most often with those we're closest to, and value the most!

Instead of barging ahead with foregone conclusions and assumptions, though, try to lead more with gentler, open-ended questions.

Here's what that looks like:

Anxiety: Worrying yourself sick about what Christmas presents to get for people.

Curiosity: Asking them! Making observations to see what they might like.

Anxiety: Telling your stubborn colleague how to fix the problem he has.

Curiosity: Asking him about what he's tried so far, and why that didn't work.

Anxiety: Ruminating about being behind in life, relative to your peers.

Curiosity: Observing the ways your life is working well for you right now, or what you might learn from others.

Anxiety: Complaining about the poor behavior of kids today.

Curiosity: Asking questions about the causes of that behavior.

Anxiety: Avoiding a difficult family member.

Curiosity: Experimenting with ways to stay emotionally regulated when with them.

Moving forward with curiosity doesn't magically resolve all your life's problems or remove everyday tensions and annoyances. What it does do, however, is put you in a frame of mind that is more able to receive:

- New solutions to problems
- Opportunities you hadn't considered before
- A fresh and unexpected encounter
- Insight and new understanding

Basically, **when we flip the anxiety/curiosity switch, we stop seeing threats and start seeing possibilities.**

When we are anxious, we are trying to control and predict.

When we are open and curious, we are willing to be surprised by something we never could have predicted.

One path leads to overthinking, the other to healthy, dynamic engagement with life.

Practice "Emotional Separation" in Real Time

Sometimes, overthinking in relationships can show up as a faulty belief that other people's experiences are somehow ours to manage.

Maybe we assume that we already know everything about our loved ones, what they will do, and what they *should* do.

Maybe we feel a slight desire to take over, as though the other person is not quite a full individual in their own right, but more of an extension of us.

Or maybe we feel highly attuned to their emotions, and take it on ourselves to regulate them, without being asked.

Here, a little emotional separation may be needed. Just because someone is having an emotional experience, it doesn't mean

- We have to match that emotion or intensity
- We have to fix it
- We have to focus on it

We can always choose to tell ourselves, "That's their business, not mine."

This may feel cold and callous, but really, it's a statement of fact. Other people have their emotions, and we have ours. Remind yourself of that by asking yourself:

"How do I want to show up right now?"

It's not as simple as just "choosing" your emotions, of course, but you do have a choice in how you play the interaction, how you hold yourself, the attitude you take, where you put your focus, what you say, and what you do.

You can hold your center even if others have temporarily lost theirs. *You* can be curious even if *they* are anxious.

Try to remind yourself that you are not being unkind or ignoring their emotions—what you're doing is declining to be *fused* with their emotions, in precisely the same way as you can choose not to fuse with your own!

Be curious, not reactive.

Stay loose and flexible.

If you do, you may notice that the impulse to overthink drops dramatically. We don't have to figure other people out, or take responsibility for them, or fix them, or convince or persuade them, or apologize for or to them.

We can just *be with* them, open and inquisitive. Ironically, it's this position that will allow us to stay engaged and connected with real compassion and understanding.

Turn to Problem-Solving

"You don't have to see the whole staircase, just take the first step."

- **Martin Luther King Jr.**

Throughout this book, we've explored different approaches, methods, and perspectives for dealing with overthinking. Which is the right one? Well, they all are!

It's as though anxiety is a many faceted gem, and as we turn it over in our hands, we can see the different surfaces. It's the same with the many different models, theories, and techniques we discuss here—it's all the same gem, we're only turning it over in our hands and considering its different facets.

In this chapter, we'll turn the gem once more in our hands and look at another side of it.

Question: What *is* anxiety?

Answer: A reaction to a perceived threat in the environment (here, we'll include uncertainty and doubt in the "threat" category).

Question: So, what happens next?

Answer: Our bodies are triggered into fight or flight mode. We resist and go to war with the perceived threat, or we escape, withdraw, or flee somehow.

Now, let's pause here. This is interesting. Our body's biological response to threat appears to be twofold. We either:

1. approach (fight)
2. run away

Question: What's missing here?

Answer: Rational problem-solving!

If anxiety is like an alarm ringing, these two responses are akin to getting angry and kicking the door down because you hate the noise, or running away so you don't have to hear the noise anymore.

A third alternative: Walk over to the alarm to see why it's ringing, and what can be done about it.

Too many of us deal with anxiety by trying to escape it:

- We drown out the alarm
- We suppress our awareness of it
- We pretend it's not happening
- We may even resort to "toxic positivity" and gaslight ourselves with

endless affirmations (has that ever really worked for you?)

But, like a warning light on a car's dashboard, it's going to keep flashing until we listen to the message it's trying to share with us.

The other extreme is to stay with the anxiety, but allow it to completely destabilize and overwhelm us:

- We fight and resist the experience
- We resort to blame and shame—for ourselves and others
- We get angry, irritated, or frustrated
- We despair, complain, or feel sorry for ourselves

And yet, for all this, the warning light is still flashing, and the alarm is still going.

Problem-solving is a life skill and a practical means to achieving self-regulation in real time.

We've spoken about anxiety as a largely false alarm, but of course, there are times when *it's activated for a reason.*

Instead of spiraling, shutting down, or going to war with overthinking, you can consciously choose to acknowledge what your anxiety is trying to draw your attention to.

Example: You're having one of those 3 a.m. existential meltdowns. Your overthinking is of the "What am I doing with my life anyway" flavor and you're spiraling out on all the big, gnarly worries.

On the one hand, you're overthinking and your current perception is exaggerated, distorted, and inaccurate. On the other hand, that first anxiety trigger may have had an important, but more moderate message for you. Perhaps the message was: "You need to challenge yourself a little more at work." or "You may have lost touch with your values."

It's precisely because you skipped over this more moderate warning/message that you hurtled on into a full-blown anxiety loop.

In this way, problem solving is a way to make use of our anxiety, and to keep it in check and in proper proportion. Our anxiety can be a **trigger** into more anxiety… or it can be an **invitation** to reflect, to create, to experiment, or to instigate concrete action.

Problem solving is the narrow, middle path. It's being able to say to yourself:

- "There's something wrong here, but not *everything* is wrong. Let's take a closer look and see what's what."
- "There's a lot going on in my mind, but let me untangle things, one thread at a time."
- "I clearly need to make some changes here, but I don't have to do everything at once, and I don't have to have everything figured out to begin."

Move at a pace that your nervous system can actually handle.

Stay grounded.

What is your attitude toward problems?

Problems are a normal part of life. When you encounter a snag, a hiccup, an issue, or a setback, what is *your* attitude?

- Feel panicked, overwhelmed, rushed, and a little confused
- Feel crushed with despair
- Get angry or annoyed
- Complain to others, dial up the drama, go into helpless victim mode, or exaggerate the problem to inspire pity and help from others
- Find someone to blame

- Quickly cover the issue up, avoid, and minimize
- Calmly focus on what you can do, and work thorough actions and consequences in a strategic, proactive way

The quality of your life does not depend on whether or not you experience problems (spoiler alert: everyone experiences problems).

Rather, it depends on *how you respond* to those problems.

It's possible to over- or under-respond to problems.

Life is full of problems, but we can choose whether we focus on the problems or the solutions.

Let's explore the *right* way to heed the true message of anxiety—the middle way—and self-regulate through rational problem solving that focuses on solutions.

Name the Trigger
We can be anxious and solve our problems *through* that anxiety.

No resistance, no avoidance, just gentle acceptance and a shift towards action-oriented, rational thinking.

If you're wired up, the alarm is activated and the warning light is flashing. Sit down and face the anxiety head on. **What's actually making you anxious?** Put words to the sensation and write it down.

Try not to overthink this, just scribble down what pops into your mind first.

When your anxiety is already triggered, it can feel like *everything* is wrong, but this is a distortion. A fire alarm can be heard all over a giant apartment complex, even though the fire is only in one corner of one small apartment. Anxiety is the same. When you're triggered, your kneejerk answer to "What's wrong?" may be an exasperated "Everything!"

But pause and try to identify exactly where the fire is. When you slow down and force yourself to put triggers down in black and white, you may be surprised to see just how trivial many of them really are:

- You came home and saw a big pile of laundry on the floor

- You felt a vague ache in your lungs when you woke up this morning
- A friend announced their baby shower on social media
- A speeding fine arrived in the mail
- The dog threw up in the living room
- Your weekend plans were suddenly cancelled due to the weather

Write these things down and take a good look at them.

There may be the temptation to blow everything out of proportion, or there may be the opposite temptation to minimize, avoid, or quickly move on in some way.

Try to find the balanced place in between: that calm, rational state of mind where you acknowledge the facts of your situation, but without holding them too tightly *or* too loosely.

Anxious and overwhelming things are normally vague and shapeless. Work against this by becoming **detailed** and **concrete**. Being **specific** about what's bothering you will help you focus on genuine issues while ignoring the rest.

Notice how the triggers above have been listed without any interpretation or implied solution.

For now it's, "Just the facts, ma'am."

So, avoid writing something like, "My lazy jerk of a roommate left a huge pile of laundry for me to do." or "Now I have to spend a bunch of money I don't have on a baby shower!"

This is racing ahead. Instead, **keep it neutral and factual.**

When your list is done, take a deep breath and identify just one thing that you'll focus on first. Your temptation might be to choose the biggest, nastiest looking issue, but instead do the opposite. Choose something that is:

- Less intense
- More actionable

Think of your overwhelm like a tangled ball of yarn. To unravel it, start to loosen the easiest, most available thread, rather than immediately pulling and tugging on the main knot.

Draw a circle around this item, underline it or even cut it out with a pair of scissors.

Scratch out or remove everything else; for now, you're focusing on this issue and this issue *only*.

Brainstorm Without Judgment

Putting things down in black and white can sometimes be soothing in and of itself. You may find that your problems look smaller and more manageable when written down, or you may find that making the list is quite overwhelming.

Both responses are normal and fine.

Both responses are part of the problem-solving process.

The next step is to start brainstorming solutions, but first, a few caveats. Try not to:

- **Rush**, force, or pre-empt the problem-solving process
    - this is simply a form of fearful control, avoidance, or escape
- **Judge** the ideas you come up with
    - this is also a fear response and not likely to help

Try setting a timer for five or ten minutes (depending on the size and complexity of the problem) and then give yourself permission to explore possible solutions in a completely open-ended way.

If it comes to mind, write it down, even if it seems silly or unlikely to work. **You're not appraising the value of solutions yet; your goal is to simply generate as many as you can.**

This is one situation in life where you want quantity over quality!

The inner critic will certainly pipe up to censor or correct you. There may also be a little voice that already knows what answer it wants you to arrive at, and it will helpfully try to steer you towards that foregone conclusion. That's normal.

However, you don't have to listen to any of this; simply ask that inner chatter to take a seat while you get on with being as creative as possible. No rushing, no judgment.

Let's imagine you've picked the baby shower trigger as the lowest hanging fruit to focus on. Your list of potential solutions may look like this:

- Handmake a gift for the mom to be
- Turn down the baby shower invitation

- Show up to the baby shower without a gift
- Offer to organize catering or decorating in lieu of a gift
- End the friendship so you don't have to go at all
- Pool money with others to buy a (cheaper overall) joint gift
- Look around for secondhand baby gifts
- Fake your own death and move to another country

The reason you're including seemingly outlandish solutions is precisely because you don't want to hem yourself in at this point. Cast a wide net. Don't make any assumptions.

Problem solving can sometimes fail for a few reasons:

- **We're just going through the motions** all the while merely talking ourselves into taking a course of action we wanted to take all along.
- **We're not genuinely brainstorming any new ideas,** we're just churning over the same old ground.
- **We're pre-censoring and pre-judging solutions** so that we don't

write something down because we've already convinced ourselves it won't work.

Give yourself time to really exhaust the possible solutions you can come up with. If appropriate, you may even call on the help of someone you trust. Only when you genuinely cannot think of anything further, move onto the next step.

Choose a Small Action and Start
This is where you can start to make judgments and appraisals. Take a look at each potential solution you've brainstormed and rank and rate:

- Which seems doable?
- Which seems likely to lead to a good outcome?
- Which solutions can be combined?
- Which solutions can be tweaked and adjusted?
- Which solution is most realistic and practical?

Pick one or two and commit to them. You don't have to completely transform your entire life, you just have to take a realistic step in the right direction.

Remember that picking an action doesn't lock you in forever. It's not a lifelong commitment. Often, you can try out a solution and come back to the drawing board if it doesn't work.

Try to be less all-or-nothing in your thinking; if something doesn't work entirely, become curious about what part *does* work, before discarding the whole idea.

It's OK to take time to work through problems, especially bigger or more serious ones.

It's OK to not have an abundance of options.

It's OK not to always like the options we have.

It's OK to find some solutions difficult.

It's OK for some problems to never really be solved once and for all. It doesn't mean we can't try, and it doesn't mean we can't make improvements.

Remind yourself that sometimes, the solution may simply be taking a short walk, breathing, grounding, and letting go. This counts!

What's important is that you're engaged in the process, and you're taking conscious action over time.

In this way, you can understand problem-solving as an indispensable anxiety-management tool. **Work on what you can, and practice acceptance and release for everything that you cannot.**

Problem Solving Affirmations
The next time you encounter a problem, pause.

Notice how you feel. Hear the alarm. Choose not to run away, nor to get fused and tangled up with the sensation, either.

Remind yourself of your agency.

Problems are normal and can be solved. When you approach them head on, they lose much of their power, regardless of the outcome. Don't let anxiety be a permanent block; chip away at it strategically.

The following affirmations can help bring you into a problem-solving frame of mind:

- "This is just a problem, and problems can be solved."
- "I can learn from my mistakes."

- "This problem is a challenge, but I also have skills, abilities, and resources to draw on to help me solve it."
- "Problems are a normal part of life. I am resilient. I know that whatever happens, one way or another I will find a way through."
- "I choose to stay curious, calm, and open-minded in the face of the unexpected."
- "This situation may be unpleasant, but I can handle it."
- "There is opportunity here."
- "I am capable. I am confident. I am strong."
- "I have solved problems like this before, and will solve this one, too."

Anxiety may be a sign—not a sign that we have too many problems in life, but a sign that we need to brush up on our problem-solving skills.

ABC Coping Sentence

"Between stimulus and response there is a space. In that space is our power to choose our response. In our response lies our growth and our freedom."

- **Viktor E. Frankl**

In this chapter we're taking a look at a super-useful CBT tool designed by therapist Dr. Claire Hayes, The ABC Coping Sentence.

This tool is not a specific sentence, but rather a *structure* or *format* that can help you contain, frame, and manage your own emotions.

By articulating and reframing your experience, you give yourself the opportunity to navigate it differently. The structure is simple:

A: **Acknowledge**. You identify and label what you're experiencing.

B: **Because**. You link up your experience to something else, so that it makes sense.

C: **Choose**. You can now consciously commit to a particular behavior that would be constructive for you going forward.

So, the format is:

"I am feeling (emotion) because (thought, event, or situation) but I choose to (helpful action)."

- When we **acknowledge** how we actually feel, we
    - Interrupt the impulse to flee or resist
    - Give ourselves the opportunity to come to accepting self-awareness
- When we add the word "**because**" we
    - Bring awareness to causal triggers and consequences
    - Validate our reactions—we're not crazy or bad
- When we **choose** what to do next, we
    - Remind ourselves that we do always have this power
    - Reorient toward the future, and what we can control

In one sentence, we have brought together realistic acceptance and acknowledgement of our true feelings as well as hope and proactive intention for how we want to move forward.

The coping sentence, in other words, helps us find that crucial *middle way*.

The Coping Sentence in Everyday Life

Non-anxious people tend to operate naturally under an implied coping sentence. With a little deliberate practice, you can learn to do the same.

Here are some examples of how and when you might pause and quickly construct a coping sentence for yourself. The technique is easy to remember and only takes a few seconds.

1. Acknowledge how you feel
2. Connect it to *why* you might be feeling that way
3. Choose your response

Eagle-eyed readers will have already noticed the overlap between Claire Hayes' method and others discussed in this book. The Choose Again Method is essentially the same technique, as is the Four Step Method—what matters here is that you are blending together an honest acknowledgement of your reality, while leaning into your power to make a new, better choice for yourself.

If we're anxious, we may get hung up on "acknowledging" our fear and doubt in an endless loop (stuck at the first step). Or we may get hung up on the fact that our feelings "come out of nowhere" and that, since they don't make sense, we ought to be ashamed or go into self-judgment (stuck at the second step). It's only when we bring everything together, and **choose forward**, that we come unstuck.

Let's take a look at some real-life examples of the Coping Sentence in action.

At work

"I'm feeling pressured and rushed right now because I have an important deadline tomorrow. But I choose to do what I can and let the rest go. <u>I choose</u> not to torture myself with perfectionism. I also commit to setting firmer boundaries for myself, so that next time, I don't accept the unreasonable demands others try to place on me."

Notice everything that is achieved with these few words:

- You are being honest and real about the anxiety you feel (no toxic positivity here!)
- You are self-validating and grounding in context
- You are not letting that anxiety control you; rather, you are empowering and encouraging yourself to make choices

that actually lower your stress, both in the short- and long-term.

During a difficult conversation with a loved one

"I am feeling defensive and insulted because I've been accused of doing something I don't believe I've done. I'm also annoyed that they don't seem to be listening to me as I try to explain myself. But I choose to remember that just because they're angry at me, it doesn't mean that I'm actually to blame or that I'm responsible for defusing their anger. I'm going to be present with them until they calm down, but I'm not going to be 'baited' by their emotion."

Before a performance

"I'm feeling totally petrified. My mind is racing and I'm all over the place! I'm anxious because I keep thinking of all the things that could go wrong. But I choose to face that fear4 and reframe it as normal excitement. I'm going to go for a run to blow off some steam, then I'm going to practice some healthy distraction to stop myself from ruminating. I'm prepared and I know it. I choose to trust in that."

Everyday overwhelm and overthinking

"I'm feeling stressed out because I'm tired. I choose to take a nap right now and recharge my batteries."

As you can see, the coping statement is extremely flexible, and can be tailored to fit *any* emotions, and *any* situation. The method doesn't tell you what to do—it reminds you that **you are always at liberty to choose for yourself**, and that means that you have far more resources available to you than you might first realize.

You can use the ABC framework to:

- Reframe unhealthy or inaccurate thoughts
- Help you ride out uncomfortable emotional states
- Carefully work through problem solving so you can take concrete steps in the right direction

Coping Sentence Mistakes

Claire Hayes' method is extremely flexible, but there are still a few ways that we can go wrong with it. Here are some pointers on creating an effective coping statement:

- **Keep it fact-based.** When you acknowledge how you feel, try to be as neutral as possible. There's no room here

for shame, blame, or judgement. Find emotion labels, and avoid letting interpretations creep in, for example:
- "I feel abandoned" (implies someone else's actions)
- "I feel like I'm going to fail" (a thought, not a feeling)
- "I feel like he's being rude" (a statement and judgment about *his* actions, not *your* feelings)

- **Steer clear of blame, shame, and conjecture**. When using "because" to explain your feeling, beware of placing blame or drawing links that are not actually there in reality, for example:
  - "...because I'm an idiot" (shame)
  - "...because of what you did" (blame)
  - "...because Mercury is in retrograde" (is this really the reason?)

- **Be realistic.** When choosing your next move, be reasonable about what is actually within your scope of control. Unrealistic expectations can end up creating more anxiety and pressure. For example:
  - "I choose to ace my exam and get a perfect score!" (really?)
  - "I choose to just get over it." (but how?)

- "I choose to have a productive, respectful conversation." (are you the only one in control of the conversation?)

Famous author and holocaust survivor Viktor Frankl never knew about CBT or Claire Hayes' approach. However, he did understand the power each and every one of us has to choose:

"Everything can be taken from a man but one thing: the last of the human freedoms—to **choose one's attitude in any given set of circumstances, to choose one's own way.**"

Choose well!

Goldilocks Principle

"Stress is like a spice—in the right proportion, it enhances the flavor of a dish. Too little produces a bland, dull meal; too much may choke you."

- **Donald Tubesing**

We've spoken about the "window of tolerance", of emotional regulation, and of the middle way between over- and under-reacting. Let's consider another metaphor now, the goldilocks principle, and see how it applies to stress.

In this chapter we'll see that **the way we conceptualize stress itself has important consequences for how we manage it, day by day.**

Let's start with a simple definition of stress.

Stress = the strain, tension, discomfort, or pressure experienced by a body and mind in the face of demanding circumstances.

A few key ideas:

- **Stress is normal.** We all experience it, and it's a part of life. We can experience stress when doing things we want to,

things we've chosen to do, "happy" things, and things that are good for us.
- **Stress is subjective**. What stresses you out might not be what stresses me out. *Your* response to stress is unique, and influenced by your history, demographics, genetics, socioeconomic factors, etc.
- **Stress is neither good nor bad**. The answer to the question of "What counts as good stress?" is "It depends."

Stress isn't automatically dangerous, but a misunderstanding of what stress is and how it works *can* be.

If we think that stress is abnormal, not subjective, and bad, then it's no surprise that we'll be stressed out about it! What's more, we'll be triggered into running away from it, fighting against it, or sticking our heads in the sand.

Here, the Goldilocks Principle can help us craft a more nuanced, balanced view of stress, and thereby help us cope with it better. According to the classic fairy tale, Goldilocks snooped around in the bears' house and discovered that extremes were never any good, but rather the moderate point somewhere right in the middle was always "just right."

With stress, we don't want too much, nor do we want too little… we want an amount that is *just right*.

That alone might have caught your attention: Is it possible to have *too little* stress in your life? Well, yes. It turns out the brain can benefit from low to moderate stress levels in short bursts:

- Preparing for an exam or performance – stress is useful nervous system arousal that you can channel into focused effort to study or prepare.
- During arguments and conflicts – stress actually improves your overall resilience and helps you learn from the situation so you cope better in future.
- When facing a fear or a trying challenge – stress provides the energy, tunnel vision, and impetus to push yourself and get over the hurdle.

Life without a little stress would feel flat, lifeless, and uninteresting. Think of how little effort you'd make on a first date if you weren't just a teeny bit stressed out about it! The stress is what *adds* excitement and thrill.

It's what makes so many human activities feel meaningful in the first place.

How much stress is too much?

Research on Adverse Childhood Experiences (ACEs) shows us that early childhood trauma can increase the chances of long-term health effects in adulthood. But the curious thing is that the healthiest and best-adjusted people are *not* those with no ACEs, but rather those with a low but non-zero score.

Why?

It's as though *a little* adversity in childhood teaches us to cope better with more serious adversity in later life. Without moderate and occasional stress, we don't have the opportunity to develop coping skills. It's counterintuitive, but a trouble-free childhood puts us at *greater* risk of buckling in the face adult adversity in adulthood (Oral et. al., 2015; Felitti et. al., 1998).

It's the Goldilocks zone again—chronic and severe stress can be extremely hazardous for the brain, whereas a small amount of time-limited stress may actually be good for it (Briere et. al., 2017).

We want to be stimulated, challenged, and activated... *not* overwhelmed, burned out and damaged. The key is finding the threshold.

Track Your Stress Range Like a Thermostat

As always, awareness is the necessary first step.

How do you feel?

Before, during, and after a tense situation, pause and rate your stress on a scale of 1-10. This is similar to the distress scale we used in the chapter on the window of tolerance:

- 1–3: Calm and focused. Tension likely to be felt as excitement or interest.
- 4–6: Slightly anxious, disconnected, or fatigued. Alert and functional.
- 7–10: You could be in or heading towards burnout zone—this is, as you remember, outside the window of tolerance and signals dysregulation.

Name your level and pay attention to how it changes over time.

If you're tracking too high, take calming measures. Hit the pause button, take a break, or do some breathing exercises to bring your nervous system back to a more manageable state.

What if you're tracking too low?

Well, don't feel like you always *need* to have stress of some kind in your life! There's a time for deep relaxation, rest, and non-activity.

However, if your low state of stress is also accompanied by

- Apathy
- Lack of enthusiasm
- Lack of motivation
- Aimlessness
- Or even depression

... then it may be time to kick things up a notch. Take a risk. Push yourself a little harder. Move out of your comfort zone and take a step towards the unknown.

Thinking about it this way, there are two types of "tired":

1. You're tired because you're doing too much
2. You're tired because you're not doing enough

Pay close attention to which extreme you're at and adjust accordingly. If you're burned out, rest. But if you're stalling, rest may be the wrong medicine. You may feel more refreshed and inspired when you make things a little more difficult for yourself.

Schedule Controlled, Short-Term Stressors
While it's essential to have a solid stress-management strategy under your belt, you also don't want to get into the habit of avoiding challenges in life or constantly playing it safe.

Learning to reframe at least *some* of your stress and worry as useful is an interesting m inset shift to make for an overthinker.

The key is to be controlled and deliberate about it. Engineer manageable, time-limited episodes of stress to cultivate more resilience. You may not initially feel like doing this, but be willing to be surprised. Often, the things we dread and predict we'll dislike end up being strangely enjoyable.

If there's a nagging task that's been weighing on you, make it a game and challenge yourself to complete the task while timing yourself. If you're afraid of public speaking, arrange to give a small, five-minute presentation. Choose the slightly harder crossword. Set the treadmill on a slightly steeper incline.

Keep telling yourself that stress is not inherently bad for you and may even have some benefits. Did you know that cortisol increases neuroplasticity? That means that being slightly stressed makes you learn faster.

IMPORTANT: Remember that helpful stress is low or moderate level—not high or severe.

Always Pair Output with Recovery

Furthermore, helpful stress is never chronic and prolonged. This is why it's important to take a moment to destress afterwards and come back to baseline. Let go, calm yourself, and feel a sense of reward.

Follow every high-focus task, no matter how small, with a reset.

Make this pause and recalibration deliberate and controlled.

It may even help to consciously tell yourself and your nervous system, "That stress was just temporary. It's over. Now is the time to rest and come back to my center."

Remember that stress is neither good nor bad. It's simply a signal our bodies send to communicate important information about our environment. This signal is sent for our own good and benefit—it exists to protect and maintain our wellbeing.

Once we've heard and responded to the signal, it can stop. We can let the stress go.

Stress is "good" if it's an accurate message from the environment that we recognize and acknowledge in good time so that we can respond accordingly. Stress is "bad" if it's an inaccurate message from the environment that we are either over- or under-sensitive to so that we fail to respond in healthy ways. Your body *can* and *will* cope with even high levels of stress and nervous system arousal if that stress: makes sense in context, is limited, is functional, and ultimately results in useful and adaptive behavior change.

But if stress is prolonged, pointless, confused, and confusing? It's likely to lead to mental and physical health problems over time, even if it's at a relatively low level.

A healthy nervous system is not one that is permanently stuck in "chill out mode." Instead, it's one that is

- **Flexible, alert, and responsive** – it can respond quickly to change

- **Resilient** – it can quickly return to baseline

Your nervous system can be flexible, nimble, and quick to respond just like any other part of your body. Ensuring that you return to baseline again after each burst of stress is a way to tone and condition your nervous system.

- If you've just done an intense sprint, finish with a leisurely walk as you allow your breathing and heart rate to settle down again.
- If you've just blasted through a challenging and cognitively draining task at work, deliberately pause for a break, or switch to a low-effort task like tidying up your desk.
- If you've just had an emotionally intense conversation, reset by lying down with your eyes closed for a moment, stroke a pet, or listen to some soothing music.

Your stress response is a normal and useful bodily system—one that you can be in conscious control of. Deliberately teach your body that stress is temporary, meaningful, and manageable.

Emotional regulation = arousal regulation

Overthinking is both the cause and the effect of a heightened stress response. The more awareness you build, and the more you practice these techniques, the more you will be able to course-correct, and make fine adjustments to your experience day by day, hour by hour, moment by moment. Your overthinking will reduce along with your stress levels.

Joy Spotting

"To experience peace does not mean that your life is always blissful. It means that you are capable of tapping into a blissful state of mind amidst the normal chaos of a hectic life."

- **Jill Bolte Taylor**

Anxiety *shrinks* awareness.

Being relaxed, open, curious, and gratitude *expands* it.

Anxiety produces a kind of tunnel vision; if there's a danger, for your own survival the best strategy is to zoom in on the threat and tune everything else out. You're hyper vigilant and ultra focused on *that one thing that is wrong in your world.*

But this strength of the brain's threat detection mechanism is also its weakness.

If you are anxious, your awareness may permanently shrink down until it really does feel like all you can see in your world are problems.

Low grade anxiety often looks like complaining.

Your threat detection system's ideal function is to scan the environment for dangers.

Chronic, low-grade anxiety, however, is not really scanning for *dangers*... it's just relentlessly picking up on tiny imperfections, snags, annoyances, dissatisfactions, and areas of lack or disappointment.

Enter the technique called "joy spotting" which is designed to counter this anxious impulse, open your awareness up again, and remind you just how many things are going right in your world.

Originally coined by Ingrid Fetell Lee, the term *joy spotting* goes beyond mere gratitude practice. Instead, it's about training your brain to have a more genuinely balanced view of the world.

Anxiety can be like a filter we lay over reality, so that eventually all we can perceive is the bad. A slight switch in perspective changes this filter, so that we allow ourselves to also take in the good, the beauty, the lightness, the awe, the joy, the sweetness, and the sheer wonder of things.

Here's the trick though:

- Anxiety is inbuilt, automatic, and hardwired. Evolution favored a hyperfocus on threat because this is what ultimately ensures survival. **Your brain has a natural tendency to focus on the bad.**
- Joy, gratitude, awe, and wonder are not automatic. There hasn't been much reason for evolution to select for joy-seeking behaviors in our species. **Your brain has a natural tendency to overlook the good.**

This means that the human *default* is to complain a little, while forgetting about the good.

It also means that if we wish to reverse the trend, we can't just wait for it to happen by itself—we need to deliberately choose to shift our focus.

It's a practice, not an instinct.

The practice is to consciously seek out the good, even in the midst of chaos, stress, or difficulty.

This not only moderates your stress response, but it changes the way you think. It doesn't cancel out your worries, but it certainly puts them into perspective. There is resilience here.

Crucially, we are not giving our brains the task of inventing things to feel good about; we are merely asking ourselves to pay more attention to the goodness that is *already there.*

Here are some easy ways to make that switch and become more aware of all the joy that is already surrounding you, right now.

Add a "Joy Cue" to Your Daily Walk or Commute

The goal of joy spotting is to intentionally seek out little glimmers of delight and appreciation in your daily life. Don't wait for a special day—find what's special about every day, just as you find it.

You're not trying to identify something rare and precious in the world; rather, you're training your awareness to notice just how special all the ordinary things really are. Those things you normally take for granted;can you look again at them, with fresh eyes?

Cultivate an attitude of

- Curiosity

- Gratitude
- Appreciation
- Surprise
- Joy
- Playfulness
- Awe

Slow down a little and look with eyes that are *expecting* to be delighted in some way. In a way, this is anti-complaining. You are actively looking for things that please, amuse, or inspire you.

Interrupt your automatic stress response. Open up your awareness. Bring balance by noticing what tunnel vision might not have allowed you to notice:

The gorgeous shade of green of a leaf bathed in sunshine…

That subtle but indescribable smell of a fresh loaf of bread…

That brief little moment of connection you felt with a friend…

Remember, that none of this is automatic. The joy is there, but we need to remind ourselves to see it!

Build in a "joy cue" to help you remember. For example, imagine that every time you put your trainers on to head out for a walk, you're also putting on your "joy spotting eyes." Set yourself the task of spotting as many beautiful things as you can. More examples:

- Every meal can be a cue to pause and anchor into your senses for a moment, as can your daily commute or bedtime ritual.
- Make travel or commuting a trigger to turn your attention outward and see the world with new eyes.
- Whenever you meet a new person, approach them as though there was a secret treasure hidden somewhere in their personality—can you find it?

Setting up these kinds of cues and triggers is not about saddling yourself with another boring task that will only become automatic with time. You're just gently prompting yourself to change your lens, open up, and wait with kind and hopeful anticipation.

Use the "First Sip Rule" During Your Next Coffee or Meal

As you sip your morning coffee or take that first bite of lunch, pause for 10 seconds.

Make a practice of committing *the first of anything* to joy, gratitude, and delight.

Pause.

Ground yourself.

Find expansiveness in the moment.

And in that expansiveness, discover an infinity of things to enjoy, relish, and wonder at. Ironically, sometimes the tinier the thing, the more profound the sense of wonderment.

Notice… whatever it is you notice. Then imagine that your own observation is itself a kind of respect and honor that you can grant the thing you're perceiving. Look with soft eyes. Be sweet in your regard for things. See the blessing in a thing's existence and be thrilled by it.

Truly, observing life in this way is a *choice* you can make.

Let the moment, whatever it is, be enough.

What about trying to see how it's even *more* than enough?

You don't have to disappear into big existential raptures. Just let the first sip, the first taste, or the first touch be a little reminder of just how rich and wonderful the world can be, once you relax out of anxiety.

Set a 1-minute Joy Timer Once a Day

The wonderful thing about joy spotting is that it creates its own kind of momentum.

What you focus on expands.

The more you choose to notice those small, delightful details, the more small, delightful details there seem to be!

Continually train yourself to redirect.

Overthinking often comes with fretting, complaining, and pessimism. Gently shift away from lack and dissatisfaction and remind yourself that there are always little sparks of energy, surprise, and happiness around you—if you will only make yourself receptive.

A great habit is to notice yourself slipping into grumbles and complaints (essentially, overthinking) and to deliberately pause. Then set a timer for one minute and see if you can find three good things about this moment you find yourself in.

- It can be sense-based (textures, sounds, colors etc.) or abstract
- It can be something amusing or funny

- It can be a moment of warmth, love, connection, and kindness
- It can be big or small, profound or silly, deep or insignificant
- It can be previously unrecognized abundance, quirkiness, or mystery
- It can be something natural or entirely man-made

You may discover two interesting things after engaging in such a practice:

- There is more good around you than you are normally aware of, and
- *The simple act of looking* for good is itself enjoyable

The anxious brain is, frankly, an ungrateful brain. It looks out onto the world with a heavy, burdened heart, sighs, and thinks wearily to itself, "This isn't enough."

Instead, train your brain to expect good things. Then you'll see them. When your awareness looks out at the world *in anticipation of finding goodness,* a little window of curiosity opens up, and for a moment the stress response is calmed.

The more you practice deliberate joy spotting, the more you'll find yourself doing it spontaneously in your day-to-day life. You may notice that moments of uncertainty or challenge don't seem quite so distressing as they might have been in the past. You may even discover a new sense of generosity in yourself, the wish to *create* joy, not just spot it.

All these things are powerful antidotes to anxiety.

This technique is easy to incorporate into other stress-reduction techniques:

- Begin a **color-walk** or similar with a little moment of joy-spotting, or simply make a point of finding joy in the little assignments you set for yourself.
- When you switch to **problem-solving mode**, take a moment to consider with gratitude the wide range of options available to you. It's even possible to find joy in your confusion: "How lucky I am that I get to grow and change in this life, and always learn new things…"
- When you run through your **3 second anxiety relief process**, snap your fingers, verbally state your name, time, and place, and then end by

noticing something that seems lovely, interesting, or encouraging in your environment.

- **In the DARE method**, when Replacing escape with approach, find creative ways to appreciate, admire, respect, or value your experience, rather than dreading and avoiding it. Ask yourself, "What good am I missing here?" Then move toward that.
- **In the Choose Again Method,** make your new choice a choice in the direction of joy, fun, awe, appreciation, or love.
- **When you replace "what if" with "we'll see",** dare to imagine that the outcome of a difficult situation may be better than you imagine, not worse.
- Whenever you notice yourself shifting out of your **window of tolerance**, instead of chastising yourself for losing alignment, find grateful joy for the fact that *you noticed and came back!*

Manage Your Cortisol

"Stress is the trash of modern life–we all generate it, but if you don't dispose of it properly, it will pile up and overtake your life."

- **Danzae Pace**

What comes to your mind when you hear the word *cortisol*?

Does this "stress hormone" seem to you like the baddie of the neurochemical bunch, the one that's responsible for all the trouble and the one you want to get rid of, no matter what?

Let's try a different frame:

Cortisol is a sophisticated chemical messenger. It's a core part of our species' ancient and finely tuned survival mechanisms.

Cortisol is healthy. It's a normal and necessary part of a functioning nervous system.

Cortisol is useful. It helps you get things done. It sharpens your cognitive processes, increases energy and motivation, and suspends non-urgent body processes so you can respond swiftly to danger.

So, where's the problem?

Our modern, man-made environment has turned this evolutionary advantage into a possible liability.

Cortisol—and the stress response system it's part of—is not inherently harmful. What is harmful is how the modern world overwhelms, distorts, and exploits that system. Our world artificially triggers our stress response, and keeps us in a state of constant, low-grade stress and nervous system arousal.

We are told that elevated cortisol levels damage our memory, interfere with our metabolism, undermine our immune system, and leave us feeling strung out and unhappy (Ghasemi et. al., 2024).

But it is more accurate to say that we suffer these things because our normal, healthy stress responses are being hijacked and overactivated by the ravages of modern life.

Cortisol is not the problem. The *chronic activation* of our stress response is.

What has stressed *you* out today?

- The relentless pressure to be productive, to do more, to keep improving
- Social media rage bait
- The "everything crisis" and a steady diet of doom in the news and media
- Never-ending economic pressures and worries
- Increasing political complexity and division
- Climate change, war, poverty
- Information overload and uncertainty
- Deadlines, notifications, and tech that never lets you switch off
- Loss of meaning, purpose, and coherent social narratives
- Everyday stressors like aging, disease, loss, and relationship struggles

Phew!

That's a lot.

Your ancestors simply didn't face stressors of this magnitude for periods this long. The physiology we inherited from them simply wasn't made to navigate the world we currently find ourselves in.

Ten thousand years ago, nobody had to do anything to moderate the influence of ultra-processed foods, BPA in plastics or gaming addiction because, obviously, these things didn't exist.

We need to think of chronic stress in the same way: not something that we were ever designed to deal with, but a disease of civilization, and a modern, man-made condition that we now have to take extra measures to mitigate.

Even though there is nothing inherently wrong with our natural responses to perceived threat, we nevertheless need to take steps to downregulate the unnatural levels of chronic stress we incur as inhabitants of the modern world.

Thankfully, our cortisol levels *can* be managed.

We can take conscious steps to reduce the influence of chronic stress in our lives, and live in healthier, calmer and more grounded ways, despite the madness of the world around us. But how?

Before we look at some easy ways to manage and regulate cortisol levels, let's do a crash course in exactly what's happening in our bodies when we feel stress and anxiety.

Your Stress Response Program

Step 1: Your brain perceives a threat.

Step 2: This perception activates the HPA axis.

Step 3: The hypothalamus receives the message first, then it relays it to the pituitary, and finally your adrenal glands are triggered to release our old friend cortisol, which enters the bloodstream and flows through every part of the body.

Step 4: Cortisol prepares the body for fight or flight:

- Glucose is quickly released to fuel fast action
- The brain's thinking becomes sharper, faster, and hyper focused (there's that tunnel vision)
- Immune responses are modulated in preparation for an attack
- Energy is redirected away from non-essential functions (like cell regeneration or digestion)

Let's pause here.

At this point, the stress response system is working *exactly as it should*. In an ideal world, the threat would pass and then you'd return to baseline.

Step 5: The cortisol is metabolized out of your system and you return to a calm, relaxed baseline state again.

Steps 1 through 4 are healthy and normal.

If we don't reach Step 5, however, we have a problem.

We stay stuck in that state of impaired glucose metabolism, permanent hypervigilance and tunnel vision, a constantly dampened immune system, and a host of body processes that are not getting the energy and resources they need, like cell regeneration or digestion.

We can run through Steps 1 to 4 a thousand times in a day—but if we constantly *complete* the process with Step 5, our mental and physical health will not suffer.

By the same token, even the tiniest "threat" in the environment can eventually kill us if it's allowed to keep us trapped in a constant, never ending state of stress.

We cannot get rid of stress.

There is no such thing as a stress-free life.

Luckly, this doesn't matter, because stress is not the problem. *Prolonged* stress is the problem. Our bodies are exquisitely designed to cope with whatever life throws our way.

That means that stress management is not about avoiding stress, but about improving our ability to *process* stress, and to routinely lower our artificially elevated cortisol levels.

The modern world does not encourage us to reach Step 5, so we need to continually find ways to bring our own nervous systems to that state, every single day.

Say it Differently When Stress Hits
How you frame things matters.

Take another look at the stress response program above. Right in the beginning, in Step 1, your brain makes an appraisal about the likelihood of danger. This is a *perception*—and a perception can be wrong.

Panic spirals and overthinking loops sometimes happen because we perceive our own panic as something to be afraid of. We reinforce and amplify the stress response when we think, "This is dangerous."

But you can halt that spiral by reappraising this cognition. We explored some ways of doing this in the chapter on the Four Step Method:

- **Relabel** the thought
- **Reframe** the meaning
- **Refocus** your attention
- **Revalue** the thought

When you notice yourself becoming stressed, remember that you have the power to halt the process by changing the way you talk to yourself.

Instead of "I have an overthinking problem, here I go again, this is bad, I'm going to give myself a brain tumor if I carry on like this, I can't believe I'm going to have a panic attack again…"

Try "This is just my body's normal mechanism for dealing with threat. My body is trying to help me. Cortisol isn't dangerous, and nothing bad is happening. My body produces stress hormones, but it's also good at clearing them away again. I can help by re-evaluating this situation in a more grounded way…"

Work in Sprints, Then Step Away
You don't have to wait until a full-blown panic attack to start taking steps to manage stress. In fact, you can **build strategic**

recovery into your everyday habits, so that you are never pushing your body to stay in a prolonged state of stress.

Your body is not a machine. It was designed for alternating periods of work and rest, effort and recovery.

When you plan your daily routine, build in plenty of time to recoup and take a breath. Your body *can* perform under intense and prolonged stress, but this should never be your default mode. In time you'll only wear yourself down.

When you work, set a timer for a fixed period (say 45, 60 or 90 minutes depending on the task) and then pause fully to give yourself a real break.

Here, a *real break* means fully and completely disengaging from effort, focus, and intensity. That means not thinking about all the stressful things you have to do once your break is over!

Sustained attention is stress. Prolonged effort is stress. Your cortisol levels will naturally rise during these moments, even if you don't feel especially anxious.

Make a point of discharging this stress, recovering, and finding homeostasis again.

If you don't, you risk compounding tiny, accumulated tensions until they result in total depletion.

Choose Movement That Calms Your System
We all know that exercise is a necessary part of a healthy lifestyle, but not all movement is created equal.

Excessive, high intensity workouts without enough rest time can quickly lead to burnout. Overexertion can exacerbate cortisol imbalance and hinder your ability to build fitness and strength, as well as make it harder to lose weight.

Alternate high intensity with moderate or low, steady-state activities that will help regulate your stress response, not aggravate it.

Go for rhythmic, comfortable exercises such as:

- Walking
- Hiking
- Swimming
- Cycling

You can also experiment with deliberately calming and soothing movement types such as:

- Yin yoga
- Stretching
- Tai Chi
- Gentle dance

Aim for consistency – regular, even, and predictable routines are inherently less stressful and taxing to the system than random chaos and sudden changes.

Stay in the Goldilocks zone – dial down effort and come back to baseline *before* you notice signs of depletion.

Keep balanced – pair every effortful exertion with a moment of rest, reset, and recuperation.

Remember: "Restore before more."

Closely Track Your Cortisol Triggers

One of the reasons that cortisol levels can get out of control is that we're simply not aware of stress building until it's too late.

Part of healthy emotional regulation means being aware of (note: not obsessed with!) the subtle changes that occur in our nervous systems moment by moment. If we can detect slight changes in tension and strain, we can step in to make small adjustments so that larger adjustments later on are not needed.

For example:

- You wake up and note that your anxiety / arousal / stress level is around a 2.
- You run a body scan and ask yourself what you need that day and plan your schedule accordingly.
- You pick up your phone, scroll for a few minutes and immediately notice the number jumps to 4. So you put down your phone again. You observe this jump tends to happen with a particular kind of content, and not others. You make a note of this.
- You have a good breakfast at a relaxing pace and perceive your level dropping right down to 0.
- Later, when you start thinking about a meeting scheduled for that afternoon, the number soars to 8. Because you're so quick to notice this, you see what the trigger really was: a particularly negative cognitive appraisal of the upcoming meeting.
- You sit down to quickly journal through this thought process, and find

a healthier alternative thought. Your anxiety goes back down to a 4.

This may seem like a lot of work, but once you become more masterful at everyday stress management, you'll do it automatically and with very little extra effort. It will be second nature to constantly pause, become aware, notice your state, and take conscious choices to adjust, realign, rebalance, and correct.

Over time, these tiny and almost imperceptible adjustments add up to a life that feels more grounded, more composed, and more enjoyable.

The less physiologically stressed we feel, the less inclined we'll be to overthink.

The less we overthink, the less we'll trigger our stress response system.

Never forget that **your body is built for managing stress.**

Surviving life's tensions and traumas is something it's made for and knows how to do. Our role is to find ways to *support* our inbuilt stress response system and help it to bring us back to rest again.

Fear-Setting

"Set aside a certain number of days, during which you shall be content with the scantiest and cheapest fare, with coarse and rough dress, saying to yourself the while: 'Is this the condition that I feared?'"

- **Seneca**

Overthinking is a little like a moon orbiting a black hole. Your thoughts go round and round and round the same axis, trapped by some kind of pull, some kind of urge to revisit the same frightening ideas… but all without ever getting *that* close to them.

A CBT therapist noticed that her client would often describe the things she was afraid of as "car crashes." She would overthink and worry about every outcome, seeing all possible endpoints as catastrophes that she could never cope with.

"I'm trying to organize this big event for Saturday, and the whole thing will just be a total car crash" she says.

One day the therapist asks her a question she isn't prepared for.

"And then what? How does the car crash look? What happens *after* the car crash?"

She was stumped. She had never really thought about what might happen after the imagined apocalypse. She had spent her entire life **overthinking** but never **thinking through** her fears in any meaningful way.

It's as though her mind ran only certain scenes from her mental disaster movie on endless loop. The car crash. The moment of loss. The big embarrassment or disappointment. Again and again she orbited this terrible moment.

Now her therapist was asking her to do something different.

Stop.

Slow down.

Follow the car crash all the way through.

Stop orbiting and just *look at* the black hole.

Tim Ferriss and Focusing on Fears

In his now famous TED talk, "Why You Should Define Your Fears Instead of Your Goals," productivity and lifestyle guru Tim Ferriss explains his method for slowing down racing thoughts so that you can pick them apart, challenge them… and move on.

His method is perfect for those of us who overthink big life decisions. It's for that "fear" of making drastic changes, reaching for our dreams or walking away from situations that are just no longer working.

Uncertainty, doubt, pessimism, and anxiety can make the banalities of normal everyday life a challenge, but they can also hold us back, preventing us from fulfilling our potential. Overthinking is one of these double problems, since it makes day-to-day life difficult while also displacing a whole world of potential growth, courage, and fulfilment.

Ferriss' exercise borrows from general CBT principles, which in turn borrow from ancient Stoic philosophy. You'll only need a few things to do get started: a sheet of paper divided into three columns, and a willingness to *approach*, rather than *avoid* your fear.

Define the Fear
Ferriss' method consists of three steps:

1. **Define** the fear
2. **Prevent** what you can
3. **Repair** the damage

The goal is to completely change your orientation towards your fear.

We already know that fear usually comes with a desire for escape, avoidance, or denial. We don't want to know anything about the scary thing; we just want to get away from it!

The first step, then, is to reverse this tendency, and adopt an attitude of curiosity and proactive approach.

To conquer your fear, you need to define your fear.

Remember that the uncertainty of the unknown is itself frightening. That means that the less you know about your fear, the more vague and shapeless and ambiguous it is, the scarier it will seem. The more power it will hold.

Don't give it that power! Instead, go deeper and ask yourself:

What exactly am I afraid of here?

What does that actually look like?

What *specific* outcomes are so terrifying?

Your mind may flinch and try to pull away, but keep looking. Follow the car crash through.

It's the worst-case scenario, yes, but what actually happens? Then what happens after that?

You're going to write all these things down in the first column. At this stage you're not trying to soothe or reason with yourself, you're just putting your fear down in black and white, and giving the nightmare a name. Start to find some shape in that nebulous cloud.

For example, you may be trapped in a stagnant and unhealthy relationship, and your overthinking is orbiting around the conundrum: should you stay or should you go? Every time you approach the idea of actually leaving, fear grips you, and you start catastrophizing. In your first column, you write:

- I'll have to endure a big, traumatic conversation that will break my heart
- Everyone will judge me for having a failed relationship and I'll be embarrassed
- I'll never find a new apartment

- I'll regret it but the damage will be done
- I'll have to say goodbye to the dog
- I'll be single forever because it's too late for me to start again
- My partner will find someone new and I'll be distraught

Take your time with this step and really exhaust your fear. Write until it feels like there's nothing further to say. In your head, catastrophes are of unknown, and therefore infinite, proportions. Just slowing down to put everything into words often makes everything seem more defined, manageable, and clear.

Shadows are frightening. **Name your fear and bring it out into the light.** Get out your tape measure and magnifying glass. See exactly what you're dealing with.

Prevent What You Can
You may notice that by simply writing out the worst-case scenario in unflinching detail, your mind loosens and starts to naturally move towards new solutions and possibilities.

You can't solve a problem that isn't clearly defined, and you can't respond to a fear that has no clear shape. But in the second column, you're going to start thinking in a practical, grounded way about your fears.

Take a deep breath and ask:

What could I do to mitigate this risk, or prevent the feared outcome from happening?

It's not true that everything is going to be a car crash. But it's also probably not true that everything is going to work out perfectly.

Real life falls somewhere in between. With a calm, rational attitude, you can navigate your way through these problems and possibilities. Remember:

You are not powerless.

You have options.

Life goes on after even the worst outcomes... and you get to choose what you do next.

To return to our example of leaving a bad relationship, you may write:

- I can always approach the break-up conversation with kindness, respect, and tact
- I have the option of asking for a break instead of completely leaving

- I can start looking into housing options now, and begin saving and planning
- I can time things well, and I can choose how and when I share the news with others

You'll recognize this as a version of the problem-solving process we've already explored—the only difference is that in this column we're **pre-empting** and **preventing**. Picking through your fears in this way will likely reveal a few things:

- Some fears are founded, and some aren't
- Some have plenty of potential solutions, some have only a few, and some may have none—we have to practice acceptance
- Some outcomes are preventable and under our control. Others simply aren't, no matter how much we overthink them

This exercise breaks down black-and-white, all-or-nothing thinking and asks you to find the nuance. You're looking at the black hole now, and you're moving through the car crash, frame by frame.

Not everything you think of in this step will be accurate, useful, or desirable, but the process of entertaining these thoughts is itself therapeutic.

Almost always, your feeling will be: "This isn't as bad as I thought."

You dial down the size and seriousness of the problem.

You dial up your capacity to cope with it.

On balance, the fear becomes normalized and more grounded in reality. Bad things can and do happen, but there is a lot you can do to improve the situation.

Repair the Damage
Let's admit that we live in the real world, where bad things do sometimes happen. What if things actually turn out as horribly as you fear?

Take a deep breath. Allow your mind to consider what happens *after* the car crash.

How would you recover?

Note that the anxious mind will not even allow you to ask this question. Why? Because the assumption is that you *won't* recover. That you can't. That's precisely why you're so afraid of this outcome—because in your mind it is just not survivable.

But have you actually considered that the worst thing could happen, and that you'd find a way through?

You could get up out of that car crash and walk away, and your life would be right there waiting for you the next morning.

Give your mind a chance to imagine life after the catastrophe. For example:

- I could move in with my friend and pay her some rent for a while
- I could go to therapy
- I could always just get another dog
- I could pay a huge amount of money to one of those fancy matchmakers that guarantee you a soul mate
- I could move to another city entirely, and start over where nobody knows me
- I could just decide not to care what anyone thinks

As you work through the post-car crash possibilities, you may notice the faintest flutter of something interesting—excitement.

The thing is, fear of big life changes is often just anticipation in disguise. When we face our fears, we realize that there is also a *best-case scenario* that we haven't fully explored. And that's exciting.

Things may not go as badly as you fear.

Take it further: Even if they do go badly, you can survive.

Take it further still: You can do more than survive. In fact, the car crash may be one of the most meaningful, fruitful, and pivotal points in your life.

Failure, disappointment, hurt, loss, and adversity:

- do not define you
- are not permanent
- will not end your world (but they may change it!)

If this final step of the process feels a little difficult, try to remember a time in the past when you overcame what felt like total disaster at the time.

- What were you afraid was going to happen?
- What actually happened?

- How bad did it feel at the time, and how catastrophic were your predictions?
- Did things turn out the way you imagined?
- What helped you to cope at the time?
- What did you learn? What insights did you gain?
- How do you see the whole episode now, after a little time has passed?

Remind yourself that your fears are seldom as insurmountable as you imagine, and that you are stronger than you give yourself credit for.

You have resources at your disposal, you have options, and your brain can help you. You only have to walk yourself *through* the catastrophe, and beyond it.

Conclusion

Congratulations for reaching the end of this book.

Before you turn the final page, let's pause to gather together everything we've learned.

In the beginning of our book, we saw that overthinking plays out on three levels:

- Overthinking is a **habit**
- That habit is informed by a **mindset**
- That mindset flows from a set of core **beliefs**

Living a balanced, grounded, and non-anxious life means adopting the right habits, mindsets, and core beliefs.

We cannot escape tension, conflict, and stress. Life is full of problems. But it does not have to be full of *anxiety*. Instead, over time we can cultivate a new, healthier set of core beliefs in the face of life's challenges:

- "Uncertainty is a part of life, but I am perfectly able to cope and thrive, and to live a happy, meaningful life anyway."
- "I always have choices, options, and resources. No matter what happens, I

am always at liberty to choose my next choice."
- "Anxiety is normal. Fear is unpleasant but it doesn't define me, and I don't have to react to it. My higher conscious self decides my life, not my fear."
- "I am not in control of everything, nor do I need to be."
- "I do not know or understand everything, nor do I have to."

On a very fundamental level, non-anxious people believe that the world is on balance a safe place, that life can be managed, and that they always have the power to self-regulate, to choose where their attention goes, to make healthy choices and to face rather than avoid fears.

And guess what?

By reading this book and applying its principles, you've taken a real step towards becoming that person.

Overthinkers possess a secret superpower. If they can reorient their focus, redirect their mental energies, and realign with their deeper values, they can become a force to be reckoned with. Their minds become powerful tools for good.

The solution to overthinking is not less thinking, but better, smarter, more compassionate, and more flexible thinking. And you can make that shift today, right now, after you read the last word of this book.

Relax.

What would it be like if you could accept life—accept this moment right now—exactly as it is?

www.ingramcontent.com/pod-product-compliance
Lightning Source LLC
Chambersburg PA
CBHW060558080526
44585CB00013B/610